Ephesians:
One Body in Christ

by
David Dockery

Adult Winter Bible Study
Convention Press
Nashville, Tennessee

PRODUCTION TEAM

WAYNE OZMENT
Editor

CAROL DEMUMBRUM
Graphic Designer

MELISSA FINN
Technical Specialist

ANGELYN GOLMON
Production Specialist

Send questions/comments to:
Wayne Ozment, Editor
MSN 172
127 Ninth Avenue North
Nashville, TN 37234-0172

MANAGEMENT PERSONNEL

BUELAH V. THIGPEN
Manager, Adult Biblical Studies Section

LOUIS B. HANKS
Director, Youth-Adult Department

BILLIE PATE
Associate Director, Bible Teaching-Reaching Division

BILL L. TAYLOR
Director, Bible Teaching-Reaching Division

This book is designed for adults. It is in the Christian Growth Study Plan, # CG-0106.

We believe the Bible has God for its author, salvation for its end, and truth, without any mixture of error for its matter. The 1963 statement of *The Baptist Faith and Message* is our doctrinal guideline. Bible quotations in this book are from the *New American Standard Bible*, copyright © The Lockman Foundation, 1960, 1962, 1963, 1968, 1971, 1973, 1975, 1977, unless otherwise stated. Used by permission.

5403-97

Contents

Highway to Heaven

You won't find it on a map, but a highway to heaven does exist. The Roman Road is explained in the Book of Romans in the Bible, and it tells how to go to heaven.

The road begins at Romans 1:16. God is the source of energy for our journey to heaven. He gives power for salvation to all who believe. We need God's power because we all have a problem with sin (Rom. 3:23). "Sin" means missing the mark, or falling short of God's intended destination for us. None of us can reach that destination on our own because all of us are sinners.

When we work, we earn money. Sin earns wages as well—wages of death. Because God loves all sinners, He has provided another route: "The wages of sin is death; but the gift of God is eternal life through Jesus Christ our Lord" (Rom. 6:23).

The highway to heaven is found in Romans 10:9: "If thou shalt confess with thy mouth the Lord Jesus, and shalt believe in thine heart that God hath raised him from the dead, thou shalt be saved." The Holy Spirit tells us we need to confess our sin and ask for forgiveness. To confess Jesus as Lord involves confessing your sin and your need for salvation. You must repent of your sin, turn away from the direction you have been going in your life. To "believe in your heart" is to place your faith in Jesus, trusting that He died on the cross to pay for your sins (Rom. 5:8).

If you would like to have salvation in Jesus Christ, pray a prayer like this one: "Lord Jesus, I confess to You my sin and my need for salvation. I turn away from my sin and place my faith in You as my Savior and Lord. Amen." Then share your faith in Jesus with a Christian friend or pastor.

Chapter 1

Spiritual Treasures in Christ

Ephesians 1:1-14

A. An Identifying Introduction (1:1-2)
B. A Sovereign Salvation (1:3-10)
C. A Holy Heritage (1:11-14)

Ephesians presents magnificent truths in highly concentrated form. Some of us have taken a long drive in the open country where road signs and crossroads are few and far between. On an easy drive like this, we can relax without concern for missing a particular turn in the road. However, to find a specific street in a congested metropolitan area, we often have to examine every street marker with great care. We must examine the Book of Ephesians carefully in order not to miss any of the important themes this majestic letter addresses.[1]

Unlike several of Paul's other letters, Ephesians does not address directly any particular error of faith or practice. However, the letter does contain implications of false teaching in the entire Asia Minor area similar to the kind that Paul addressed more specifically in his Letter to the Colossians.

The Letter to the Ephesians beautifully portrays the themes of reconciliation and church unity. From heaven to earth, Paul showed how Christ has torn down the walls of separation and alienation to bring us together with God. Paul wrote to expand his readers' vision so they might understand more clearly the dimensions of God's grace and eternal purposes. Paul wanted his

In Ephesians, Paul emphasized God's purpose to unify all things in Christ. Your study of this letter can help you become a more vital part of God's redemptive activity.

5

readers to appreciate and to worship the God who has called the church into being through Christ.

What barriers separate members of your church and Christians in general? How can you help remove the barriers?

An Identifying Introduction (1:1-2)

Ephesians is one of the great books of the New Testament. It has been called "the crown of St Paul's writings,"[2] "the Queen of the Epistles,"[3] and "the greatest . . . and most relevant of his [Paul's] works."[4] The late W. O. Carver, the great Southern Baptist Seminary professor, observed that Ephesians is "the greatest piece of writing in all of history."[5] Christians throughout the ages have followed the sentiment of John Calvin and have recognized this Pauline letter as their favorite portion of Holy Scripture.[6] It

ILLUSTRATOR PHOTO/ BOB SCHATZ (12/2/1)

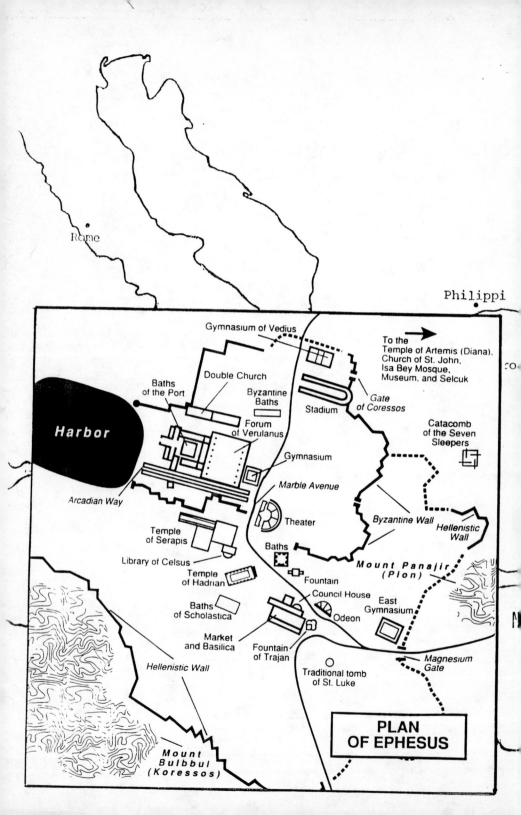

Rome

Philippi

Gymnasium of Vedius

To the
Temple of Artemis (Diana).
Church of St. John,
Isa Bey Mosque,
Museum, and Selcuk

Double Church

Baths
of the Port

Byzantine
Baths

Stadium

Gate
of Coressos

Harbor

Forum
of Verulanus

Catacomb
of the Seven
Sleepers

Gymnasium

Arcadian Way

Marble Avenue

Theater

Byzantine Wall

Hellenistic
Wall

Temple
of Serapis

Baths

*Mount Panajir
(Plon)*

Library of Celsus

Temple
of Hadrian

Fountain

Council House

East
Gymnasium

Baths
of Scholastica

Odeon

Market
and Basilica

Fountain
of Trajan

Magnesium
Gate

Hellenistic Wall

Traditional tomb
of St. Luke

**PLAN
OF EPHESUS**

*Mount
Bulbbul
(Koressos)*

certainly is the most majestic portrait in God's Word of the church and of the unity of God's people.

The Author and the Recipients (1:1)

The grand Letter to the Ephesians begins with a self-identification of the writer (v. 1): "Paul, an apostle of Christ Jesus by the will of God, to the saints who are at Ephesus, and who are faithful in Christ Jesus." Paul, the apostle to the Gentiles, wrote the letter (see Acts 9:15; Eph. 3:1).

Initially, Ephesians probably was intended to be a circular letter, sent to other churches in addition to the one in Ephesus. Paul may have written it about the same time he wrote Colossians and Philemon (about

Your town or city is significant because the people who live there are important to God. How can you share God's love with people who need to know of His care for them?

The silt delta where the sea used to come to the port at Ephesus.

A.D. 60-62) while he was evidently in prison (3:1; 4:1; 6:20). This imprisonment was most likely in Rome.

Even though the letter probably was intended for other churches in Asia Minor as a circular letter, the more prominent recipients were likely the believers at Ephesus.[7] Ephesus was the most important city in western Asia Minor (present-day Turkey). Ephesus was an intersection of major trade routes in a most significant commercial center. It had a harbor that opened into the Cayster River, which in turn emptied into the Aegean Sea. Ephesus boasted a pagan temple dedicated to the Roman goddess Diana (Acts 19:23-41; Diana is the Latin name for the Greek goddess Artemis). Paul recognized the importance of having a strong church in Ephesus. He made Ephesus a center of his evangelistic efforts for an extended period (see Acts 18:19-21; 19; 20:13-31). The church there apparently flourished for some time, though not without need for additional exhortation (Rev. 2:1-7).

Paul identified himself as an "apostle" (Eph. 1:1). An apostle was a person gifted by the Holy Spirit whom the resurrected Christ commissioned and sent on special service. Paul was carrying out that apostolic commission according to "the will of God." Paul lived under God's authority, a theme stated throughout his writings.

The theme of grace that runs through each section of Ephesians grows out of Paul's dramatic conversion on the Damascus road (see Acts 9:1-31). Prior to his conversion, Paul was an enemy of Christ breathing out murderous threats against the Lord's disciples. Paul had been immune to the Christian proclamation and immensely satisfied with his ancestral faith.

Yet, the heavenly vision and the voice that Paul experienced confirmed to him that he was encountering the risen Lord (Acts 9:3-5). The reply must have been almost unbelievable for Paul when he heard the words: "I am Jesus whom you are persecuting" (Acts 9:5). Following these words, Paul received further directions that eventually resulted in a complete reorientation.

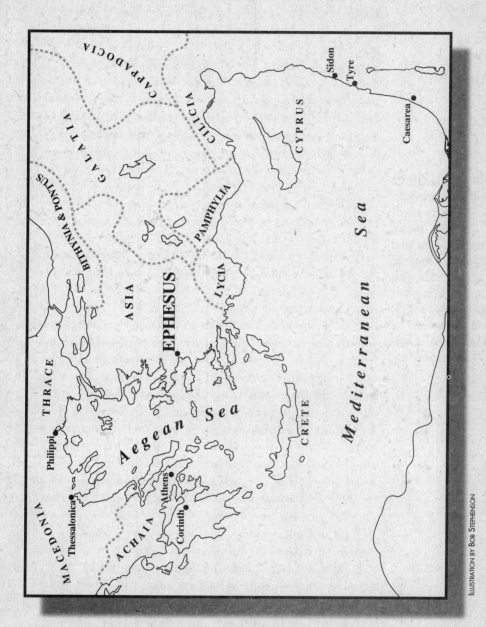

Map of New Testament world showing location of Ephesus

Paul began to understand that in spite of his zeal for God's law, his previous life was under God's judgment. A voice from heaven had corrected him, and nothing more was to be said. Jesus, whose followers Paul had persecuted, indeed was alive and exalted. Paul had come to understand that Jesus' death on the cross did not discredit His claims to messiahship. Instead, Jesus' death fulfilled prophecy. Jesus was God's provision for sin, and His resurrection confirmed Him as Lord (Eph. 1:7,20-23; 2:1-10).

Because Jesus is Lord, an unbreakable unity exists between Christ and His people (Eph. 4:1-6). Even though Paul thought he was persecuting Jesus' followers, in reality he was persecuting the risen Christ. Thus, Paul came to recognize that he had a mission to carry out for Christ (Eph. 3:2-13). The experience on the Damascus road formed the background for Paul's entire life of mission, including his ministry to the church at Ephesus (Acts 19:1—20:1; 20:17-38).

Jesus identifies with His people. He is present with them, working in and through them to realize His purpose. He gives grace, strength, and direction. He also shares their suffering.

Paul's conversion experience provided the theological foundation that shaped his letters as well as his proclamation. All of Paul's inspired writings reflect an overwhelming gratitude for God's grace in Christ, but none more than the Letter to the Ephesians. We need to recognize the importance of reading Paul's Letter to the Ephesians as an inspired word from God. Whenever we refer to Paul's thoughts or words in this letter, we should observe that God's Spirit breathed out the words (see 2 Tim. 3:16-17); therefore, the words are as truthful and authoritative for us as they were for the original readers and hearers.

Paul did not address the Letter to the Ephesians merely to citizens in Ephesus but to the "saints" (Eph. 1:1), the members of the believing community. "Saints" are holy ones—people who have been called, set apart to Christ. All persons who have repented of their sin and placed their faith and hope in Christ are saints.

10

The Greeting (1:2)

Every society has its own way of writing letters. In our modern western world, we begin letters with the address "Dear _____" and conclude by signing our names. The custom during Paul's time differed from ours. In Paul's society, people had the sensible habit of beginning with the writer's name. This was followed by "to (the name of recipients)" and words of greeting. Conforming to this custom, Paul followed normal letter-writing patterns of his day with what we might call an A-to-B greeting (Paul to the church).[8]

To the normal greeting, Paul added the words "grace to you and peace from God our Father and the Lord Jesus Christ." This was Paul's normal greeting that he Christianized for his readers. He took a customary greeting of his day and infused it with Christian meaning. Instead of the word for *greetings* (*charein*), he used the word for *grace* (*charis*). Grace precedes peace because peace results from God's grace. Peace implies fellowship and reconciliation with God (see Rom. 5:1). It also can mean experiencing God's peace in our lives (see Phil. 4:6-7). Grace and peace are God's gifts and are repeated themes in Ephesians. Paul used the word "grace" 12 times and the word "peace" 8 times.

Following the greeting in 1:1-2 is a sequence of statements about spiritual blessings that belong to the church in Jesus Christ. All of these marvelous blessings flow from God's grace, wisdom, and eternal purpose. Paul emphasized that we have received salvation not only for our personal benefit of having relationship with God but also in order for us to praise and to bring glory to God. The fulfillment of God's purpose is to bring all things together under Christ's headship and lordship (see 1:10). Paul prayed for believers to gain an understanding of God's purposes, grace, and love (1:15-23; 3:14-21). In doing so, the apostle recognized that

> How does your awareness that in Christ God has forgiven you affect your daily living? Verbally or in writing, express gratitude to God for His grace.

People want peace—inner peace, peace with others, and a wider peace that makes their world safer. Often, they have in mind serenity, absence of conflict. Biblical peace is wholeness under God's rule, a spiritual health that comes in relationship to Him.

11

only the Holy Spirit's work can open and illuminate believers' eyes to these great truths.

Central to the message of Ephesians is the re-creation of God's redeemed family according to His original intention for humanity at the time of creation. The new creation destroyed the misguided view that God accepted the Jews and rejected the Gentiles. Paul claimed that this distinction was abolished at Christ's sacrificial death. Thus, no more hindrance remains for reuniting all humanity as God's people with Christ as the Head (1:22-23). God has endowed the new body, the church, with the Holy Spirit's power. He has done so in order to enable the members to live out their new life (1:3—3:21) and to put into practice the new standards of the Christian community (4:1—6:20). In summary, the overall emphasis of Ephesians is the church's unity in Christ through the Holy Spirit's power.

> Believers are members of God's family. In the margin, list benefits of being a member of His family. Then list responsibilities of being a family member.

A Sovereign Salvation (1:3-10)

Ephesians 1:3-10 is the first part of one long sentence in the Greek New Testament that runs from verse 3 to verse 14. The section often is called "the doxology" because it recites what God has done and is an expression to Him of worship, praise, and honor. Similar doxologies are in 2 Corinthians 1:3 and 1 Peter 1:3. In this majestic section (1:3-14), Paul wrote of the blessings that belong to the church through the Father, blessings that have come through the Son, and blessings we have through the Holy Spirit.

The section 1:3-10 deals with important salvation themes such as redemption, adoption, election, predestination, union with Christ, and the Spirit's sealing work. Some of these ideas are difficult to understand, but we must not allow that to deter us from recognizing the spiritual richness of this passage.

Blessings in Christ (1:3)

God has blessed us with all of the blessings
in the heavenly realms. These blessings include our union with Christ; being seated
with Him in the heavenlies; and our
adoption, redemption, and election. All
spiritual gifts and service abilities also
flow out of these spiritual blessings that God
gives to every believer at the time of salvation. Paul
began his letter from the divine and the eternal perspective.

When Paul proclaimed that God has blessed believers
with blessings from the heavenly realm in Christ, he referred to God's graciousness and to the extent of His
kindness toward us. As a result, God is worthy of
praise and thanksgiving. The phrase "the heavenly
places" refers to the divine realm in which the resurrected and exalted Christ now reigns. We are to view all
matters relating to life and salvation from that perspective, for they are worked out in and from that realm.
God's eternal purposes are carried out from this realm.
Through our union with Christ, we already have been
made beneficiaries of every spiritual blessing.

The key phrase in 1:3 and in the initial section 1:3-14
is "in Christ." This was Paul's favorite phrase or idea.
The phrase and kindred phrases occur 10 times in 1:3-
14 to describe our union with Christ. Union with Christ
is the invisible faith relationship believers have with
their Meditator, Jesus Christ. It represents our acceptance with Him, but it also goes beyond that. In a
sense, this spiritual union goes beyond our ability to
understand and to explain. Christ in us is "the hope of
glory" (Col. 1:27). Believers are the "faithful in Christ
Jesus" (Eph. 1:1). God's grace makes possible the union
and the continuing relationship.

Paul's phrase "in Christ" emphasizes that the realm or sphere in which believers live is Christ. They share His life, and they receive from Him the resources they need to live victoriously.

Election in Christ (1:4)

The idea of divine election that Paul addressed in 1:4
flows out of the important theme of spiritual union, for

Stones at Delphi with inscriptions about freeing of slaves

election is "in Christ." The doctrine of election is one of the most central and one of the most misunderstood teachings of the Bible. At its most basic level, election refers to God's plan whereby He accomplishes His will. Election encompasses the entire range of divine activity from creation to the end time, the time when God will make the new heavens and the new earth.

The theme of election is grounded in the Old Testament revelation that out of all the earth's peoples, God chose to make Himself known in a special and unique way to one particular people. The meaning of election is best understood as God's sovereign initiative in bringing persons to faith in Christ, resulting in a special covenant relationship with Him. The early Christians saw themselves as heirs of Israel's election (1 Pet. 1:2; 2:9). Paul treated election as a recurring theme in his letters. He used both a noun form ("choice" Rom. 9:11; 11:5,28; 1 Thess. 1:4) and a verb form ("choose" Eph. 1:4). The theme serves as a foundation to the entire opening section, Ephesians 1:3-14, which includes the phrases: God "chose us" (v. 4); "He predestined us" (v. 5); and "having been predestined" (v. 11). The idea of election has been God's way in history since Abraham's time.

Paul's pointing to the Christ-centered character of election is vitally important for us. God chose us in Christ before the foundation of the world. We cannot understand predestination or election apart from this important truth.

We are elected to a holy character and to a godly purpose (1:4). God elected us to bring glory to Him (1:12). Our election results in a response of worship because we recognize that our salvation is totally God's work. Yet, we always must recognize that God uses such means as prayer, preaching, witnessing, and the Spirit's work to accomplish His elective work. Recognizing that God uses human means to bring about His divine elective purposes answers many questions relating to election.

Some people think that election results in a fatalistic mind-set of what will be, will be; thus, human participation and responsibility are eliminated. However, because God requires human repentance and faith we cannot equate election with fatalism. Some people have questioned the need to proclaim the gospel if salvation is tied to our election. Again, we must recognize that God has chosen preaching as the means to awaken faith in the hearers. The church's responsibility is to proclaim the gospel to everyone, knowing that only God's Spirit can convict us of sin and bring about faith.

When we accept Christ as Savior, we are set apart for His service. We also are to be morally pure, upright—without spot or blemish. In serving Him, we are to live exemplary lives that draw others to Him.

15

Some people have contended that election results in the kind of prideful mind-set that Israel had. This never should be the case if a person really understands election. Our election is not a pretext for pride but an opportunity for humble service.

Only when we understand the true meaning of God's elective purposes do we recognize our involvement in His redemptive mission. God chose us "from the beginning for salvation through sanctification by the Spirit and faith in the truth" (2 Thess. 2:13). This being the case, the proper response to election is not pride but gratitude for God's amazing grace that saves eternally. The doctrine of election provides confidence during times of trial and doubt. It leads us to praise God for His great grace.

The New Testament consistently emphasizes God's initiative in our salvation. At the same time, equally clear evidence exists that we are responsible for responding to God's initiative. The New Testament does not offer a formal discussion of the problem of reconciling God's sovereignty with human free agency. However, the New Testament does not leave the issue in doubt. God certainly will call a people for Himself who will be presented faultless before His throne. This underscores one of the deeper truths of the Bible: God is as gracious as He is sovereign. This gives strong grounds for assurance and is the foundation for Christian service.

Baptists always have been divided over the issue of election, and the present situation is no exception. Some people stress the unconditional nature of election in line with historic Particular Baptists like Andrew Fuller, William Carey, and Charles Spurgeon. Others emphasize the human response and articulate a conditional concept of election

In what ways are you allowing God to use you to further His redemptive purpose? How can you influence others for Christ?

Have you responded to God's invitation to salvation? The article on page 4 offers help for responding positively.

16

in line with the English General Baptist Thomas Helwys.

Earnest followers of Christ have viewed the doctrine of election differently. Some have chosen to stress the human element and a conditional understanding of election; others have maintained the divine initiative of unconditional election. That all Christians ever will agree fully on an answer to this question this side of heaven is doubtful. However, we can agree that God is the Author and the Finisher of salvation; and like Wesley and Whitefield, we can acknowledge our differences without breaking fellowship with one another. Instead, we can concentrate on proclaiming the gospel of God's grace to a lost and needy world.

Paul's concern in his missionary activity was to take the good news to lost people. God is the sole Source and Mainspring of all redemptive action, but He is not the sole Actor. God is the only efficient cause of salvation, but He is not the only participating factor in salvation. We are not robots that God manipulates, yet salvation is totally God's work. Salvation is not merely a self-determined human response, yet we must respond. We must maintain the sovereignty of grace and at the same time affirm human responsibility. Only people who are transformed by divine grace can make a positive response to God's gracious invitation, but only people who make such a response actually are transformed by grace. Far from violating our wills, God's grace appeals to our deepest yearnings. Thus, when we are exposed to grace, we are drawn to it. The ultimate purpose of this important teaching is to give the credit to whom it belongs: the gracious God who has saved us!

How has God expressed His grace to you? Out of what motive do you serve Him?

Notice what Paul stated regarding the outcome of our election. We have been chosen so that we can be "holy and blameless" (Eph. 1:4). This teaching motivates us toward holiness, which is the mark of election. Holiness and blamelessness are the results, not the basis, of God's election.

17

Gracious Adoption in Christ (1:5-6)

In 1:5 Paul stated that all of God's blessings are in accord with a purposeful predestination. This means that God's actions are purposeful and grounded in love. Through God's purposeful love, we are adopted into His family. Adoption is the legal declaration that we are God's children with all of the rights, privileges, and duties belonging to believers. This work of adoption is according to God's will and purpose. It is more than regeneration (the new birth), though the two terms are related closely.

Adoption is grounded in God's glorious grace. Salvation is God's free gift, and in no way can we merit it. Grace declares that salvation is not the result of our quest for God but of God's initiative toward us. Paul especially made clear that grace comes while we are still in our sins (Eph. 2:1-10; Rom. 5:1-11). Grace is God's free favor to the undeserving. We are given grace, not because we deserve it, not even because God could see that we would believe, but simply because God is gracious.

> God adopts believers through "the kind intention of His will" (v. 5). What other evidences of His kindness have you experienced?

Redemption in Christ (1:7-10)

> Paul took the word "redemption" from the slave market of his day. He used it to convey the truth that believers have been set free from sin's enslavement by Christ's self-giving. We could not free ourselves; only God's work in Christ could do so.

Verses 7-10 focus on Christ's redemptive work. Redemption means that we have been bought with a price (1 Cor. 6:20; 1 Tim. 2:6; 1 Pet. 1:18-19). We are redeemed from sin, Satan, and the misery of self (see Col. 2:13-15). Redemption involves setting us free, which we could not do for ourselves. We need a Redeemer because we cannot help ourselves out of the miserable state of being apart from God. Verse 7 identifies the price of redemption: Christ's death, identified as "His blood." Redeemed people are believers, persons whom God has adopted and accepted into His family. The result of redemption is a sending away of our sins resulting in forgiveness. The teaching of redemption is central and primary to understanding this passage. The basis of redemption is grace. Grace is for all people, but not all people choose to receive it.

In 1:8-10, Paul emphasized the gifts that accompany redemption, including future blessings and insight into the mystery and the fulfillment of God's will. Redemption involves more than past election and present forgiveness; it also includes a future hope and transformation.

Verses 8-10 indicate that God's grace has been "lavished upon us" in accord with the "mystery of His will." Paul did not mean that God's will is secret like the teachings of the mystery religions of Asia Minor. *Mystery* means "the revelation of something previously concealed so that it now can be understood" (see 3:2-13). In 1:9-10, the mystery involved the fulfillment of God's will, "the summing up of all things in Christ" (v. 10).

> In light of God's generously lavishing His grace on us, what should be our response?

The goal of history is based on God's divine purpose concerning the crucified Redeemer, Jesus Christ—for whom, through whom, and in whom are all things. The goal is to establish a new order of which Christ is the acknowledged Head (see 1:22). Christ is the Head of a reunited universe. He now rules and reigns from God's right hand. One day He will establish His kingdom and bring in the new heavens and the new earth, fulfilling and finalizing God's redemptive purpose. This is what is involved in "the summing up of all things in Christ, things in the heavens and things upon the earth" (1:10).

A Holy Heritage (1:11-14)

In 1:11-14, Paul saw the end result of redemption from the standpoint of eternity past to eternity future. First he answered the question, "Who will receive the holy heritage?" The recipients of the possession are people whom God has chosen and predestined. Again Paul built on the Old Testament theme that the new people, the elect ones, are in continuity with the covenant people of the Old Testament (see Deut. 7:6; 32:9; Ps. 33:12). Next, Paul answered the question of the source of this heritage by pointing to God's will. Believers do not become God's possession by chance or coercion but by grace with the enabling of God's Spirit.

The Holy Spirit was promised (Joel 2:28-29; John 14:15-26; 16:5-16; Acts 2). He is described as a seal (showing ownership like a brand) and as a pledge (a down payment, an engagement ring). I remember the excitement that Lanese, my wife, and I shared when I gave her an engagement ring as a pledge of my love to her. Though we were not married yet, we looked forward to a life together based on our mutual promise of love. Likewise, the Spirit's work is inward in the believer and shows that though we have not yet experienced redemption in full, God will bring about final redemption (life in His immediate presence) for all who have received the Spirit (v. 14). Thus, our inheritance is guaranteed.

> What evidences does your life give that the Holy Spirit is working in you? In what ways will you cooperate with Him as He seeks to move you toward spiritual maturity?

[1]Throughout the book I have followed the exposition/illustrative approach in R. Kent Hughes, *Ephesians: The Mystery of the Body of Christ* (Wheaton: Crossway Books, 1990); and Warren W. Wiersbe, *The Bible Exposition Commentary*, vol. 2 (Wheaton: Victor, 1989), 7-62.

[2]J. Armitage Robinson, *St Paul's Epistle to the Ephesians*, 2d ed. (London: James Clarke & Co., n.d.), vii.

[3]William Barclay, *The Letters to the Galatians and Ephesians* in *The Daily Study Bible Series* (Philadelphia: The Westminster Press, 1958), 83.

[4]John A. Mackay, *God's Order: The Ephesian Letter and This Present Time* (New York: The Macmillan Company, 1964), x.

[5]W. O. Carver, *The Glory of God in the Christian Calling: A Study of the Ephesian Epistle* (Nashville: Broadman Press, 1949), 3.

[6]John Knox also especially must have treasured it, for on his deathbed the great Scottish reformer frequently had read to him Calvin's sermons from Ephesians. A reading of *The Pilgrim's Progress* suggests that John Bunyan received much of the inspiration for his famous allegory from Ephesians. A study of hymnals indicates that the language of Ephesians forms the basis for many of the songs used in our worship. See introductory comments in Curtis Vaughan, *Ephesians: A Study Guide Commentary* (Grand Rapids: Zondervan Publishing House, 1977), 9.

[7]See Craig S. Keener, *The IVP Bible Background Commentary: New Testament* (Downers Grove, Ill.: InterVarsity, 1993), 541.

[8]See Andrew T. Lincoln, "Ephesians," vol. 42 in *Word Biblical Commentary* (Dallas: Word, 1990), 4.

● ● ● ● ● ● ● ● ● ● ● ● ● ● ● ● ● ● ● ●

Chapter 2

A Prayer for Friends

Ephesians 1:15-23

A. Prayer of Thanksgiving (1:15-16)
B. Prayer of Intercession (1:17-23)

Immediately before World World II in a small south-western town, a fire broke out in the neighborhood school; and many children died in the fire. Scarcely a family in town was not touched by the terrible tragedy. During the war, the town remained without a school building. When the war ended, the town—like many others—began to rebuild and to expand. One of the first items on the town's agenda was to build a new school with a sprinkler system that would prevent a fire such as the previous one from ever taking place again. When the school was completed, the town was extremely proud of the new building.

Honor students were selected to guide citizens and visitors on tours of the new facility to show them the finest, most advanced sprinkler system technology could supply. Never again would such a tragedy visit the town. The population continued to grow, and again the town had to enlarge the school. When the construction crew began the work to add the new wing, the workers discovered that the new sprinklers never had been connected properly. What an unbelievable story! Yet it mirrors the tragedy that happens in many Christian lives. Ephesians 1:15-23 indicates the power that is available to every believer in Christ, but many believers fail to connect with the power source.

> **Much of our praying is asking something from God. Petition is valid; but so is gratitude, praise, and intercession. Our praying needs to be well-rounded. Paul's prayers can be instructive to us.**

21

For the switch to turn on the light bulb, it must be connected to a power source.

How can we connect with God, our primary power source, on a consistent basis? What steps will you take to receive God's power daily?

In 1:3-14, Paul completed his song of celebration expressed in a lengthy sentence that praised God for the believers' blessings in Christ: divine election, redemption, salvation, and the gift of the Holy Spirit. Though that sentence ended, Paul's celebration did not. He turned to thank God for the Ephesian church's faith and love.

Prayer of Thanksgiving (1:15-16)

Our expressions of gratitude to fellow believers for what they mean to us can affirm them, encourage them, and deepen our relationship with them. Expressions of appreciation can strengthen the bonds of fellowship and can enhance ministry.

In most of Paul's letters, his customary thanksgiving followed his salutation. In the Letter to the Ephesians, his lofty words of blessing intervened. In 1:15 he began an expression of gratitude that is a part of a prayer of intercession.

Paul's prayer of thanksgiving for the believers' spiritual progress arose out of what he had written in 1:13-14. Thus, he began with the words "for this reason," a transitional phrase. Most likely Paul wrote and sent the Letters to the Ephesians, the Colossians, and Philemon at the same time. Philemon 5 indicates that Paul recently had received word about the faith of the believers in the areas of Asia Minor.

22

Paul particularly was thankful for two things: his readers' faith and love. Faith finds its focus in Christ and expresses itself in love to others. Such love is the evidence of genuine faith (Gal. 5:6).[1]

Faith in Christ

Paul expressed thanksgiving and praise to God for his readers' faith in Christ. They had been saved by grace through faith and not by their own effort (see 2:8-9). Paul also offered thanks for their practice of faith. The church members not only rested their eternal salvation on Christ, but they also rested their everyday living on Him. They trusted Christ to take care of them through every aspect of life. Paul's prayers in their behalf were continual. He went on "giving thanks for" and "making mention of" their "faith" and "love." "Making mention" involves specifically remembering them—actually mentioning them by name before God. This serves as a model to us about how specific and regular our prayers are to be.

Evaluate your praying. Are your prayers specific or general? Do you pray for people in general, or do you call persons by name? Do you ask forgiveness for specific sins?

Love for Others

Paul not only gave thanks for his readers' faith but also for their exemplary love. The word "all" (v. 15) is significant. They loved all of their fellow Christians. Surface Christianity may arm us with what we think are proper prejudices and a rationale for criticizing people who fall short and who disagree with us. We are able to keep them at arm's length. Unfortunately, this is often the case in Christian circles; but it was not true of the Ephesian believers!

Paul thanked God for the Ephesian Christians' thoughtful and purposeful love that willed to love even the unlovely—the same kind of love that God has for us. We are to live out the kind of love that Jesus modeled and commanded when He said, "A new command-

Christian love, *agape*, is not a warm feeling for others. It is a determined goodwill that seeks the best for others no matter how they respond. *Agape* is not discouraged easily but goes on offering itself even when people reject it.

ment I give to you, that you love one another, even as I have loved you, that you also love one another. By this all men will know that you are My disciples, if you have love for one another" (John 13:34-35).

When faith and love are paired, we have something for which to thank God. We likewise need to thrill and to rejoice when we hear of others' faith and love. Often, instead of praising God for others' love and faith, we experience envy and jealousy. We are resentful when others are praised. Paul's attitude turns this around. True, only people who are thankful for others' spiritual achievements can pray for them. So Paul's celebrating heart moved from praise to petition. How should we pray for people we love? Look at Paul's beautiful example of prayer in behalf of others.

Prayer of Intercession 1:17-23

The Ephesian Christians dared to believe and to act on their faith. Often, the reason we do not do the same is our lack of knowledge. We are not aware of the spiritual wealth that God has made available to us through Christ. We are too much like the late newspaper publisher, William Randolph Hearst, who invested a fortune collecting art treasures from around the world. Mr. Hearst once found a description of some valuable items that he felt he must own. He sent his agent to find them. After a lengthy search, the agent reported that he had found the treasures. All along, they had been in Mr. Hearst's warehouse. The newspaper publishing giant had been searching frantically for treasures he already owned! Had he read his own treasure catalog, he would have saved himself a lot of money and trouble.[2]

What spiritual resources has God made available to you? Which are you using to enrich your life and to strengthen your service? Which are you not using?

Paul wanted the Ephesian believers to understand what great spiritual resources were theirs in Christ. Paul knew of their faith and love, and in this he rejoiced. Then he prayed for their spiritual enlightenment. Paul made four requests: that the Ephesian believers might know and experience God, that they might know the hope of their calling, that they might know of God's glorious inheritance, and that they might know of God's great power. Paul wanted his readers to know God's power as it is exhibited in Christ's resurrection, exaltation, reign, and lordship.

To Know and Experience God (1:17)

Paul addressed his prayer to the only One who is capable of answering this kind of intercession—the same One who is worthy of all praise (see 1:3). Paul presented God as glorious (v. 17) and powerful (v. 19). Glory and power are aspects of His divine nature and activity.

Paul prayed that the Holy Spirit might empower the church fully. God had given believers the Spirit, who had sealed them. This sealing guaranteed their inheritance until the day of their ultimate redemption. In 1:17, Paul prayed that they would be endowed with the spiritual powers of wisdom and revelation. Revelation or vision refers to the insight and the discernment the Spirit brings to the mysteries of divine truth. Paul wanted his readers to have a spirit of wisdom so that they might get to know God more completely. One of the great expressions of the Christian faith states that the goal of the Christian life for people is "to know God."[3] A further statement suggests that a person's chief end is to "glorify God, and to enjoy Him for ever."[4] That goal is based on Paul's prayer for knowledge of God in Ephesians 1:17. The Greek word translated "knowledge" means the fullness of knowledge acquired through personal acquaintance and experience. God already has given believers wisdom and insight (1:8-9), but Paul interceded for the church not only to understand but to experience these blessings.

How well do you know God? What steps will you take to know God better? How can you experience God to a greater degree in your daily living?

To Know the Hope of Their Calling (1:18a)

In verse 18, Paul used an unusual metaphor: "the eyes
of your heart." This phrase refers to inner awareness.
The heart is the seat of moral and spiritual insight.
Paul wanted believers to realize that God has made
available to them magnificent heavenly blessings. The
first is "the hope of His calling." This phrase refers to
the assurance of eternal life guaranteed by the possession of the Holy Spirit.

To Know of His Glorious Inheritance (1:18b)

Paul also wanted his readers to understand "the riches
of the glory of His [God's] inheritance in the saints."
This phrase points to the truth that believers will inher-
it all of God's blessings (see 1:3,11,14; Rom. 8:32).
Particularly at this point, Paul was concerned about
the believers' heavenly inheritance.

The Greek expression, like the English, could mean
either God's inheritance or ours; that is, either the inheritance God receives or the inheritance He bestows.
The Old Testament consistently taught that God's people were His inheritance. This statement is likely in line
with the Old Testament understanding.
Thus, Paul's idea was that the inheritance
was the wealth that God sees and will realize by being glorified in His saints.

*What are the implications of
the idea that believers are
God's inheritance? How
should this concept affect
our daily living?*

"Inheritance" also could refer to the
glorious inheritance that the
Christians come to experience
through salvation. Exactly what this
inheritance will be like is beyond our
ability to understand or even to imagine.
Certainly it includes the experience of transforming
worship. God's inheritance for us will not be a little
private party for each individual. It will be for all of
the saints who make up the people of God—believers
from every nation, tribe, people, and tongue who stand
before the throne and before the Lamb (see Rev. 7:9).
Paul apparently did not think we are presumptuous to

contemplate our heavenly inheritance. In fact, he encouraged us to anticipate it with joy and gratitude.

To Know of His Great Power (1:19)

The fourth aspect of prayer focuses on the enabling power needed for Christian living. If the "calling" looks back to the beginning and the "inheritance" looks forward to the completion or fulfillment, then surely God's great power spans the present period in between. Because this particular blessing focuses on present living, Paul concentrated his prayerful attention on this matter. Only God's power can fulfill His people's expectation. His power alone can bring us safely to the riches of the final inheritance's glory that He will provide for us in heaven.

What encouragement and motivation does your assurance of a heavenly inheritance give you?

Paul knew that God's power is sufficient, and he emphasized this truth with an abundance of words to convince his readers. He wrote not only of God's power but also of "the energy of the might of His strength" (Greek text). Paul prayed that believers might know the immeasurable greatness of God's power. In doing so, he employed an unusual Greek word translated "surpassing." The term *huperballon* [hu per BALL on] means "something belonging to another sphere altogether" ("transcendent"). Paul built on this word to add all of the synonyms he could bring together to talk about God's power, working, strength, and might.

The Greek word translated "power" (*dunameos*) [do NA me ohs] points to capability or potential. The term rendered "working" implies effective power. The word for "strength" refers to power that is supreme, superior, victorious; and the word for "might" points to vital power, muscular force, or inherent ability. The point is that the extraordinary, divine power by which Christ was raised from the dead is the same power at work in and through believers. This startling truth certainly extends beyond the normal experience of most Christians.

Our society is intoxicated with the quest for power—political, corporate, religious, and personal. Much of the quest is ego-driven. The power God makes available for Christians is power to live as He intends—refining character, coping with difficulties, and influencing people for Christ.

27

Resurrection Power (1:20)

Christ's resurrection was the driving force in Paul's life. Death is a vicious and a relentless enemy (see 1 Cor. 15) that will attack all of us one day (see Heb. 9:27). John Stott told about being called to visit a member of his church who had been taken to a hospital in an emergency. Stott had expected she would be near death when he arrived, but instead he found her sitting up with a smile on her face. She told him that when she was brought in, the medical staff gathered around her as if she were about to die. Then she added that she decided not to die! Certainly her remark was spirited, wrote Stott, but not entirely true. To succeed in postponing death is sometimes possible, but we cannot escape it. No human power can prevent death, let alone bring back to life a dead person.[5]

What is impossible for humans is possible for God. He raised Jesus from the dead. First, He arrested the natural process of decay, refusing to allow His Holy One to see corruption (see Ps. 16:10; Acts 2:27). In raising Jesus from the dead, God did not merely reverse the process but transcended it. He raised Jesus to a completely new life, giving Him a resurrection body that no one before had experienced and that no one has experienced since. However, the Bible declares that all true believers also will receive a resurrected body at Christ's return (see 1 Cor. 15).

Paul wrote that God's power effecting Christ's resurrection is available to believers. If we do not have that power, why not? How can we receive it? In the margin, write two ways you will begin to live more fully by God's power.

Some Christians have attempted to reinterpret the resurrection by saying that Christ has risen in our hearts; that is, Christ did not rise in any literal sense but only in the faith of our proclamation. Nothing could be farther from biblical truth! Paul's statement in Ephesians 1:20 emphasized God's displaying His divine power in what actually was accomplished in Christ, not merely in His followers. However, Paul's point was that God's resurrection power is available to believers!

Paul ascribed Jesus' resurrection to the Father; yet, the Father and the Son were at one in the miraculous act. Thus, Jesus could claim in John 10:18 that He had authority to lay down His life and to raise it up again. Paul wrote that not only was Jesus raised, but He also is seated at God's right hand (see Ps. 110:1, a favorite Old Testament verse of the early church). The right hand of God is the place of authority from which Christ now reigns.[6]

Christ's Exalted Authority (1:21)

In verse 21 Paul wrote that Christ is seated "far above all rule and authority and power and dominion, and every name that is named, not only in this age, but also in the one to come." The Greek term translated "far above," like that used for "the heavenly places" (literally, "the heavenlies"; see 1:3,20), is not a spatial term or even a dimensional expression. It indicates Christ's superior position. He is above all angelic powers, including whatever supernatural beings Paul's readers might have had in mind. Christ is above all of them. Angels were thought to control humans, but Christ controls human destiny and angelic activity with absolute authority because He is infinitely superior.

In what ways do you acknowledge Christ's authority in your life?

The phrase "every name that is named" refers to all authorities in any time period: Paul's, ours, or the age to come. Christ is above them all. Whatever anyone wants to name so-called powers, Christ is superior to all of them.

The Role of Christ's Headship (1:22-23)

Paul stressed Christ's exaltation in the conclusion of his prayer. All things are placed under His feet (see

29

Ps. 8:5-6; the words describing humans were applied to Christ). Hebrews 2:6-9 shows that the destiny of all things is in Christ's power. He is the Head who rules over the church, but He also rules over everything. We might have expected Paul to write that as Head over everything, Christ is the Head of the body. Instead, he wrote that Christ in His exaltation over the universe is God's gift to the church (see Col. 2:10). The church has authority and power to overcome all opposition because its Leader and Head is Lord of all.

Christ's ascension and exaltation complete the resurrection. They also provide hope for believers as Christ becomes the first fruit of His people. As the first of the harvest, He guarantees the final redemption and exaltation of people who are in union with Him (see 1 Cor. 15:23; Col. 1:15-18).

From the exalted right hand of God, Jesus carries out His ministry of intercession for His people. He dispenses the gift of His Spirit to enrich and to enable the church to carry out its mission. Most of all, our Lord's accession and exaltation indicate His superiority above everything.

Christ is Lord of the church, His body. Only when this becomes the church's operating principle can it move toward fulfilling its mission and purpose. The goal of seeking Christ's will and of pleasing Him must take priority over personal preference.

We must not miss the point of Paul's prayer. If we want to know Christ better and to have the knowledge for which Paul prayed in verse 17, then we must understand and believe the glory of His exaltation. Not only this, but Paul wrote that our Lord wants us to be with Him. Jesus prayed in His high priestly prayer: "Father, I desire that they also, whom Thou hast given Me, be with Me where I am, in order that they may behold My glory, which Thou hast given Me; for Thou didst love Me before the foundation of the world" (John 17:24). What an astounding truth for the church (see Rom. 8:18-39)!

Finally, the ultimate significance of all that Paul wrote in Ephesians 1:17-23 lies in the final verses of this section that describe the church as "His body, the fulness of Him who fills all in all" (1:23). Paul referred to the church as Christ's body (a favorite term of Paul in Ephesians; see 4:4,12,16; 5:23,30). In earlier letters Paul had used the term "body" (see Rom. 12:4-5; 1 Cor. 12:12-27), but not with the sense of Christ as the Head. In Ephesians 1:22-23, Paul claimed the church exists and functions only by reason of its vital relationship to its Head, who is Christ.[7]

The declaration that the One who leads the church is somehow filled up by the church is one of Paul's great tension-filled statements: "the fulness of Him who fills all in all." Paul often followed this tension-filled pattern when he wanted to think deeply about a great truth. How can this be? As the resurrected and exalted Christ, He is without need and is independent of anything. Yet as Head, He is incomplete without the body. Thus the church, as the body, is part of that which fills up Christ. So the body and the Head are one in the truest sense. This is an astounding wonder, that unless He is united to us, the Son of God is in some measure incomplete. John Calvin said, "What an encouragement it is for us to hear, that, not until He has us one with Himself, is He complete in all His parts, or does He wish to be regarded as whole!"[8]

As a member of Christ's body, how can you help the body function more smoothly? In the margin, write two actions you will take to enhance your church's health and effectiveness.

[1]See Leon Morris, *Expository Reflections on the Letter to the Ephesians* (Grand Rapids: Baker Book House, 1994), 29-30.

[2]The story is told by Warren W. Wiersbe, *The Bible Exposition Commentary*, vol. 2 (Wheaton: Victor, 1989), 14.

[3]Thomas F. Torrance, ed. and trans., "The Catechism of the Church of Geneva" in *The School of Faith: The Catechisms of the Reformed Church* (New York: Harper & Brothers, 1959), 1.1.

[4]Thomas F. Torrance, ed. and trans., "The Westminster Shorter Catechism, 1648" in *The School of Faith: The Catechisms of the Reformed Church* (New York: Harper & Brothers, 1959), Q.1.

[5]John R. W. Stott, *God's New Society: The Message of Ephesians* (Downers Grove, Ill.: InterVarsity Press, 1979), 58-59.

[6]See Peter Toon, *The Ascension of Our Lord* (Nashville: Thomas Nelson Publishers, 1984), 15-17.

[7]D. M. Lloyd-Jones, *God's Ultimate Purpose: An Exposition of Ephesians 1:1 to 23* (Grand Rapids: Baker Book House, 1979), 426-28.

[8]John Calvin, *Calvin's Commentaries: The Epistles of Paul the Apostle to the Galatians, Ephesians, Philippians and Colossians,* trans. T. H. L. Parker (Grand Rapids: William B. Eerdmans Publishing Co., 1965), 138.

Chapter 3

Spiritual Transformation

Ephesians 2:1-22

A. Old Life (2:1-3)
B. New Life (2:4-10)
C. New Oneness in Christ (2:11-22)

One of the most common mistakes in our time is to think of evangelism more in terms of a method than a message. Such sometimes is the case with revivalists or evangelists who have suggested that evangelism can take place only when persons responding to a gospel invitation say the right words or pray the right prayer. Recently, some people have taken this thinking so far as to suggest that evangelism can take place only when the right music is played or the right songs are sung. What has been lost, or at least misplaced, is the recognition that accompanying genuine evangelism must be a firm theological foundation. Evangelism is the proclamation of the good news in words and the manifestation of this good news in deeds with the purpose of reconciling people to God. The focus of Ephesians 2 is God's good news and the reconciliation that Christ has accomplished.

God not only has raised Christ from the dead by His mighty power, but He also has raised from the dead the people who have trusted Christ as Savior. The idea of

> In what ways are you involved in sharing the good news of Christ? In what additional ways could you be involved?

32

rising with Christ is not new in Paul's letters (see Rom. 6:1-14). In other places, however, rising with Christ is the sequel to death with Christ and burial with Him. The pattern is different in Ephesians. The death from which God has made us alive with Christ is not our death with Christ. Our resurrection is from our moral and spiritual death that has resulted from our sinfulness. In Ephesians 2, Paul contrasted our condition as new persons in Christ (vv. 4-10) to our former condition apart from Christ (vv. 1-3).

Old Life (2:1-3)

Many people have hiked to the top of Mount Whitney in California, the highest point in the lower 48 states (14,495 ft.). From this high point a person can see for miles the beautiful sights all around. Less than 80 miles to the southeast of this beautiful peak is Death Valley, the lowest spot in the United States at 280 feet below sea level. It is the hottest place in the country, with summer temperatures reaching well over 100 degrees in the shade. What an incredible contrast between the cool air on the top of Mount Whitney and the relentless heat at the bottom of Death Valley! In Ephesians 2:1-3, we get a glimpse of the Death Valley of the soul before Paul's words take us to the peak to see the heavenly realms in Christ. The contrast between the two natural points enhances our appreciation of the difference between our life in Christ and the life that characterized us before we placed our faith in Him.[1]

One powerful way we can share our faith is to give our testimony of our experience with Christ. We can tell of our life before we trusted Christ, how we became a Christian, and what life has become since we accepted Christ. People need to hear our story.

Without Life (2:1)

Apart from Christ, people are without spiritual life. Paul defined this as "dead in . . . trespasses and sins." The most vital part of human personality is dead; thus, people cannot experience fellowship with God or meet His requirements. This is true because people are sinners who have transgressed the law. "Trespasses" are lapses; "sins" are shortcomings.

Are sins of attitude as severe as sins of actions or of omission? Why or why not?

33

These are evident in our lives in many ways including acts, thoughts, and desires.

Without Freedom (2:2)

Paul described the former way of life as literally, "You walked about according to the course of this world." The walking was in accordance with this age—the ways of this world. "This world" is associated closely with the realm of Satan. The expression "the prince of the power of the air" points to the atmosphere as the abode of demonic spirits. Satan is the leader of these wicked spiritual hosts. He is the unholy spirit who seeks to undo and to counterfeit God's work. The phrase "is now working" is literally "the one now operating," which points out Satan's deliberate deceptive schemes. Sinful people are in the bonds of Satan and are without freedom. They are children "of disobedience." Apart from Christ, all people are in rebellion against God because of their refusal to believe in Him.

The phrase "sons of disobedience" (2:2) is a Hebraic way of indicating a lifestyle. The Hebrew language had no adjectives; so the phrase "son of . . ." indicated what a person was like. Unsaved people are marked by disobedience to God.

Without Hope (2:3a)

Paul also affirmed that people who are apart from Christ are without hope and under divine wrath. Paul wrote in verse 3, "we . . . all" also "formerly lived" among them (the children "of disobedience"). The Greek word translated "lived" is a different term from the one in verse 2 translated "formerly walked," though the idea is similar. The word in verse 3 means "to turn to and fro and behave in accordance with certain principles." Thus, Paul declared that not only Gentiles but also everyone is bound in sin's grip. Apart from Christ, people are dominated by the "flesh." "Flesh" is not merely the body. The Greek term as Paul used it described an orientation away from God toward selfish concerns. The word translated "indulging the desires of the flesh" has a negative meaning,

In the margin, list temptations of the "flesh." What resources do Christians have to help them resist the pull of the flesh?

34

and the plural suggests multiple unredeemed urges in
our life apart from Christ. The unredeemed person is
completely at the mercy of the tyrant self and its lustful
impulses. As a result, all people deserve God's punish-
ment (see Rom. 1:18—3:20). This condition is a result
of our choosing like Adam chose (see Rom. 5:12-21),
which is in contrast to the state of grace described in
Ephesians 2:4-10. Apart from grace we are condemned.

The Impact of Sin (2:3b)

The entrance of sin into the world has had great and
negative influences on all God's creation. The negative
impact has been especially great on the human race
that God created in His own image. As a result of sin,
God's image was not lost (Gen. 9:6; Jas. 3:9); but it is
tarnished and marred severely. Sin's effects on humans
and on the course of nature have disturbed drastically
the role of exercising dominion that God gave people at
creation (Gen. 1:28). The ability to live in a right relationship with God, others, nature, and ourselves has
been corrupted. All attempts at righteousness are as
filthy garments in God's sight (Isa. 64:6). All people
apart from Christ are spiritually dead and are alienated
from God. Therefore, they are unable to reflect properly the divine image and likeness.

The fall into sin described in Genesis 3 was not merely a moral lapse but a deliberate turning away from
God in rejection of Him. The day that Adam and Eve
disobeyed God they died spiritually, which ultimately
brought physical death. Sin's entrance has brought
about a sinful nature in all humanity that Paul described in Ephesians 2:3 in the words "by nature children of wrath." Thus some Bible students deduce that
people are not simply sinners because they sin; they sin
because they are sinners. Other Bible students contend
sin entered human history with Adam and Eve's sin,
and we become sinners by willfully choosing their path
of rebelling against God. People act in accord with their
natures. None of us ever act contrary to our nature.

35

Sin has affected adversely our responsibility to be good stewards of God's creation. God gave us dominion—not the right to use and to abuse earth's resources as we decide but to manage those resources responsibly. Most often, greedy consumption has replaced awareness of a God-given privilege and responsibility.

The idea of our sinful nature is most significant when we reflect on our relationship to God. Because of sin's entrance into the world and our following Adam's sinful nature, we are by nature hostile to God and estranged from Him. We have wills that do not obey God, eyes that do not see spiritually, and ears that do not hear spiritually because we are dead to God. While we function as free moral agents, sin always affects our decisions and actions. In day-to-day decisions, we have the ability to make free and rational choices; but our sinful nature always influences those choices negatively. We do not genuinely repent or turn to God without His enabling us to do so because we are "by nature children of wrath." Thus, before Paul began his proclamation of the good news of reconciliation, he made sure his readers understood the problem of sin.

An awareness of the problem of sin helps clarify frequently misunderstood concepts about the nature of sinful humanity. Our nature is depraved, but this does not mean that we are as wicked as we can be. Rather, depravity means that sin negatively impacts all aspects of our being. People still can and still do perform right and good things as society views them; but some of these thoughts and actions may be sinful by God's standards. We can affirm that people choose to do good but not the ultimate good that is the goal of pleasing God and seeking His eternal glory. Thus, depravity involves our total willful rejection of God's will and glory.

We are totally depraved, but we cannot say we are totally corrupt. Other factors—such as environment, emotional makeup, heritage, and the continuing effect of our having been created in God's image—influence degree of corruption. Yet, all types of immoral actions— whether lying, murder, adultery, seeking after power,

What ministries can you, your Sunday School class, and/or your church perform in your community that will honor God and will influence people for Him? List one such ministry in the margin and begin to take steps to implement it.

homosexuality, pride, or failure to love one another—
are aspects of our sinfulness, depravity, and alienation
from God. The human heart is wicked, corrupt, and
deceitful (Jer. 17:9). The degree of wickedness, corruption, and deceitfulness differs from individual to individual and from culture to culture; but certainly some
people are more noble than others. Still, all people
without Christ are estranged from God.

The biblical answer to people's dreadful situation is
that Christ has provided a way to reconcile us to God.
God's grace has provided restoration for believers and
has brought about a right relationship with God, one
another, nature, and ourselves.

In light of God's
mercy and grace
to us, Christians
are to become
progressively
more merciful
and gracious.

New Life (2:4-10)

The strong contrast begins with the word "but" (v. 4).
Over against the human rejection of God, Paul painted
a picture of the Author of the new life manifested in God's gracious acceptance of sinners because of Christ. God could decide
to condemn all of His creation and still
remain consistent with His righteousness. Instead, His great love led Him
to show mercy and grace.

Do you most often look for
flaws or negative qualities
in people, or do you look for
positives and possibilities?
What steps will you take to
begin to look for the good
in others?

God's Great Mercy (2:4)

Mercy is God's compassion for the
helpless that relieves their situation.
Mercy is God's not giving us what we deserve;
grace is His giving us what we do not deserve. Love is
the divine disposition that sees something infinitely precious in people in spite of their sin. Thus Paul could
write that God, "being rich in mercy, because of His
great love with which He loved us," made us alive with
Christ. God's loving heart contains an inexhaustible
treasury of mercy. God's loving mercy moves Him to act
on behalf of the world. He not only makes new life possible; but He also shares it with us because He has
made us alive, raised us up, and seated us with Him.

37

Resurrection Life (2:5-6)

In verse 5, Paul described the basis of the new life. His description is an extension of the thought in verse 1. He described what God has done in Christ for every believer. When believers were spiritually dead in "trespasses and sins" (2:1), God gave them new life together with Christ. The life Christians now have is a result of Christ's resurrection power. Believers' resurrection and regeneration are an act of God's grace. Paul viewed salvation in retrospect from the vantage point of redemptive history. Thus he could write we are in a position of having been saved (*sesosmenoi* [ses ohs MEN oi]).

In verse 6, Paul pictured the condition of the new life. God has raised us up with Christ (see 1:20-23). This is an act of God's great power that has enthroned us with Christ in the heavenly places, even as Christ was exalted to God's right hand following the resurrection. Elsewhere, Paul described the reality of the struggle of the Christian experience (see Rom. 7:14-25; Gal. 5:16-25)—what we may characterize as three steps forward, two steps back. But Paul's point in Ephesians 2:6 was to draw contrasts between the human condition described in verses 1-3 and the new life pictured in verses 4-6. This is exemplified by the strong contrasting words in verse 4—"but God"—and can be seen in the following chart:

What does your being enthroned with Christ mean to you? What assurance does it give you? What demand does it place on you?

Old Life	New Life
We were dead.	Now we are alive.
We were enslaved.	Now we are enthroned.
We were objects of wrath.	Now we are objects of grace.
We walked among the disobedient.	Now we fellowship with Christ.
We were under Satan's dominion.	Now we are in union with Christ.

These truths are almost too glorious to comprehend! Again we see the reason Paul prayed that the eyes of our hearts might be opened to understand what God has done for us in Christ. Our salvation is a display of divine grace. God did all of this in Christ with a single goal in view: to demonstrate the surpassing wealth of grace (2:7). This was God's publicity program, the exhibition of His favor for all of history to see, including angels as well as people (see 1 Pet. 1:10-12).[2]

Reconciled to God (2:7-10)

Paul described the work of reconciliation with four key terms in verses 7-10: (1) "kindness"—love and tender action; (2) "grace"—God's free favor toward ill-deserving people (a favorite term of Paul that he used more than 100 times); (3) "faith"—the instrument that brings us empty-handed to God (see Rom. 10:17); and (4) "salvation"—in Ephesians 2:8 ("saved"), equated with the new life, forgiveness of sins, deliverance (from our plight described in 2:1-3), liberation, and resurrection.

Note the emphasis in verse 8 that salvation is "by grace . . . through faith." The work of salvation is for God's glory and is not accomplished by human works. The whole process of salvation is not our achievement but is an act of God's goodness.[3] The emphasis is always on Christ, the object of faith, not on the amount of faith.

Salvation is not a result of anything we have, anything we have done, or anything we can do. Any kind of self-effort is ruled out by the expression, "not as a result of works, that no one should boast." The phrase prevents the slightest self-congratulation or boasting. Salvation is by God's completely unmerited favor; boasting is out of place. In the Greek text, the grammatical construction of the entire phrase "by grace . . . though faith" serves as the antecedent of the phrase "it is the gift of God" (2:8). We cannot understand grace as God's part and faith as our part, for all of salvation is a gift from God.

> The Greek word translated "kindness" is extremely close to the word "Christ." "Kindness" conveys gentleness and benevolence. God delights in showing kindness to us; we are to display this attitude toward others.

39

Examine more closely the meaning of faith. The Bible maintains that faith is the means by which we receive salvation. Faith includes a full commitment of the whole person to the Lord Jesus, a commitment that involves knowledge, trust, and obedience. Faith is not merely an intellectual consent or an emotional response; it is a complete inward spiritual change that the Holy Spirit confirms to us. God brings about faith, and faith is the human response that produces complete submission to God and full liberation from the snare of sin. The object of faith is not as much the teaching about Christ as it is Christ Himself.

What areas of your life do you need to submit to God?

Though faith is more than doctrinal ascent, it must include adherence to doctrine. In our belief in and commitment to Christ, we acknowledge Him as Savior from sin and as Lord of our lives (see Rom. 10:9), even Lord of creation. True conversion definitely involves a personal belief in Christ as the God-Man and in His work as Savior. However, we must remember that a person may have a correct knowledge of Christ without a living faith in Him!

The work of our salvation is a display of divine handiwork (2:10). Paul never intended verses 8-9 to be read apart from verse 10. We were dead; now we are God's workmanship, His work of art. This is a display to the watching world and an evidence of grace. Works are the fruit of salvation, not the cause of salvation. Now that we are united with Christ, we are to be like Him, for He went about doing good.

Good works are not incidental to God's plan; they are an essential part of His plan. Good works are in sharp contrast to the "walking about in the ways of this world" and "following the ruler of this world" that we formerly did (v. 2, author's translation). We demonstrate our good works in gratitude, character, and actions. Grace does not encourage sinful living (see Rom. 6:1-11); it encourages living in freedom and in righteousness.

40

God accomplished His marvelous salvation by what Paul described in Ephesians 1:7 as Christ's redemptive work. The idea of redemption is vitally related to the themes of liberation, deliverance, and ransom. Paul understood the struggle between the kingdom of God and the hostile powers that enslave people. Redemption is bringing sinners out of a hostile bondage into authentic freedom (see Col. 2:15). As Redeemer, Jesus breaks sin's power and creates a new, obedient heart by purchasing us from the power of sin, guilt, death, and Satan (see 1 Pet. 1:18-19).

God made possible our salvation. He has created us; and in Christ, He has re-created us. He created us out of nothing; He has liberated us out of bondage and has resurrected us out of death. We now are new persons whom He has forgiven and released from sin.

In the margin, list good works you will do to demonstrate God's work of grace in you.

New Oneness in Christ (2:11-22)

In verses 1-5, Paul considered his readers' moral and spiritual condition before their conversion to Christ. Then he reminded them of their previous religious and social deprivation from his vantage point as a Jew. Notice the emphasis on "you" in verses 11-13,19-22 and on "we" or "our" in verses 14-18. Many people think that verses 14-18 served as a confessional statement or as a hymn that was used widely in the early church.

Understanding the structure of verses 11-22 can be helpful for our interpretation. We can view this section from three perspectives: (1) corporate condition apart from Christ (vv. 11-13); (2) corporate reconciliation in Christ (vv. 14-18); and (3) new standing as God's new humanity (vv. 19-22). The theme of this entire section is reconciliation. The idea of reconciliation involves bringing fallen humanity out of alienation (separation) into a state of peace and harmony with God. Jesus, as Reconciler, heals the separation and the brokenness that sin creates and restores communion between God

We must be careful concerning our motive for doing good works. Jesus said we are to do good deeds in order to glorify God, not to draw people's praise (Matt. 5:16). People are to see the Father who prompts the deed, not the person doing the deed.

and people. Reconciliation is not a process by which people become more acceptable to God but an act by which we are delivered from estrangement (separation) to fellowship with God. Because of Christ's work on the cross, God has chosen to treat believing people as children rather than as transgressors (see 2 Cor. 5:18-20; Col. 1:20-22).

To whom do you need to be reconciled? What steps will you take to effect reconciliation?

Apart from Christ (2:11-12)

"Therefore" (v. 11) refers to the entire previous section (vv. 1-10), which is one sentence in the Greek text. Not only were the Gentiles morally separated from God (vv. 1-3), but they also were separated from God's people. They were an underprivileged group—pagans. They were separated from God's covenant people. Jews thought Gentiles were fuel for the fires of hell. Gentiles thought of Jews as social barbarians. The distance between the groups was immeasurably great.

The Gentiles' heathen state was one of spiritual bankruptcy. They were without any knowledge of Christ. They had no rights in God's family and were not recipients of God's covenants. They were without hope. Ultimately, they were without God. Paul did not reproach the Gentiles for their plight. He recorded the sad truth of the matter.

Reconciliation in Christ (2:13-18)

Paul always phrased reconciliation in terms of our needing to be reconciled to God through faith in Christ. God, the offended party, took the initiative to bring us to Him.

Quickly and eagerly, Paul turned to the Gentiles' new relationship in Christ. He moved away from their tragedy and alienation to the joy of their reconciliation in Christ. Paul used the strong transitional phrase "but now" (v. 13). The Gentile believers no longer were in their alienated state. They knew Christ, took part in God's covenant blessings, and had hope and fellowship with God. This turnaround took place "in Christ" (v. 13). People who trust Him have a present salvation and a future hope.

42

People who were far away had been "brought near."
This phrase describes the position of Gentiles and Jews
from a Hebrew mind-set. The phrase "far off" may be a
reflection of Isaiah 57:19 in which the prophet referred
to Jews who lived "far" from the temple in Jerusalem.
Paul used the phrase to indicate spiritual separation
from God and His covenant blessings.

The phrase "He Himself" (v. 14) emphasizes the cen-
trality of Christ in bringing Gentiles and Jews together,
not only with one another but also with God. Christ
alone has solved the problem of our relationship with
God and with other people. He is both our peace and
our Peacemaker. This truth is more than a message
about Him. Jesus' reconciling work that His death on
the cross accomplished has made the two—Jews and
Gentiles—into one. Gentiles do not become Jews, but
the two groups become one—the church. The new humanity is greater than the former humanity. God has
removed the hostility, and He has broken down the hatred forever.

Paul described hatred and hostility as a
barrier, a dividing wall. Bible students
have given various explanations of "the
dividing wall." Some interpret it as an
illustration of the intense difference
that separated Jews from Gentiles.
Others see a Gnostic idea of a wall dividing heaven from earth and its being broken down by an ascending savior. Still others understand the dividing wall as recalling the common
rabbinic idea that the law was a fence separating Jews
from all other races and thus creating hostility. The
most likely explanation is to understand the phrase as
used by Josephus, the great Jewish historian. Thus it is
understood best as the area in the Jerusalem temple
that separated the court of the Gentiles from the
temple.[4]

The temple was constructed on an elevated platform.
Around it was the court of priests. East of this was the

What artificial barriers separate people in our world?
What one barrier will you
work to remove?

court of Israel. Farther east was the court of women.
These three courts were all on the same elevation as the
temple. From here a walled platform was five steps
away. Fourteen steps away was another wall, which was
the outer court of the Gentiles. Warning notices were
posted in Greek and Latin (discovered in archaeological
digs in 1871 and 1935) that read: "No man of another
race is to enter within the fence and enclosure round
the Temple. And whoever is caught will have only himself to thank for his ensuing death."[5]

The warning did not state that trespassers would be
prosecuted; it declared that they would be executed.
Paul envisioned Christ's demolishing this wall at the
cross, though it was not destroyed physically until the
destruction of Jerusalem in A.D. 70. Paul had been ac-
cused of violating this standard in the account in Acts
21:28-29. This incident probably led to the imprisonment where he found himself while he penned this letter.

What does the phrase "broke down . . . the dividing
wall" mean? Suggested meanings are: (1) The law was
made ineffective; (2) cultural demands had ceased; (3)
the whole law had been done away with; or (4) doing
away with the specific commandments that separated
Jews from Gentiles because Gentiles did not observe the
Jewish law.[6] The last option seems best,
whether we understand the "dividing
wall" as a barrier in the temple area or
symbolically as a fence around the
law. In either case, the burden of the
commandments ("enmity," v. 15) was
taken away at the cross in our
Lord's crucified body. The result is a new
humanity that is not a hybrid but a new creation,
a new race.

What do you think would happen if Christians saw themselves as a new creation, a new race?

The Greek word translated "reconcile" (v. 16) extends the concept of peace and involves the idea of
restoration to a unity. The goal was not merely to reconcile two groups but to reconcile them together to

44

God. The "one body" (v. 16) is the church, the new humanity, the place of peace. At the cross, everything that meant disunion was destroyed.

The preaching of peace in verse 17 is the Spirit's work through the church in obedience to Christ's commission. Notice the priority of Gentiles in verse 17. Historically, the gospel first went to the Jews (see Rom. 1:16); but in Ephesians 2:17 Paul gave priority to the alienated Gentiles.

Access to the Father is available to all people who come to Christ (v. 18). "Access" carries the idea associated with an oriental court official who conducted visitors into the king's presence. Thus, through Christ's reconciling work we have been ushered into God's presence.

PHOTO BY LEO DE WYS

"He . . . broke down the barrier of the dividing wall" (Eph. 2:14).

New Humanity (2:19)

Two interesting terms are in 2:19: "strangers" (*xenoi* [ZEN oi]), which means short-term transients—nonresident foreigners—with no rights, and "aliens" (*paroikoi* [PAR oi koi]), which means resident foreigners who had settled in the country of their choice and who had limited rights. These two terms describe the Gentiles' position before Christ. Two additional terms picture their new position. In Christ they were: "fellow citizens" (*sumpolitai* [soom po LI tie]), which refers to people who enjoy all the privileges of "God's household" (*oikeioi tou theou* [OI kie oi too the oo])—another way to describe their togetherness and inclusion. The last two phrases indicate that believers are adopted into God's family and are united with the saints of the past as well as with all other believers. In ancient times, the household was what we today would call an extended family. This new family is God's new family.

God's new family, the church, is not only a new nation and a new family but also a new building. In verse 20, "foundation" conveys the idea of a solid structure. In 1 Corinthians 3:11, Paul referred to Christ as the foundation. In Ephesians 2:20, he stated that the apostles and the prophets in their unique relationship to Christ are the foundation. The apostles' and the prophets' importance and uniqueness are clear. Today, the work of pastors and teachers cannot be equated with the roles of apostles and prophets.

Paul proclaimed Christ as the cornerstone of the foundation. "Corner stone" (v. 20) refers to a capstone or a binding stone that holds the entire structure together. It was a corner right angle joining two walls, and I suggest that the royal name was inscribed on it. In the world of Paul's day, I think it was considered even more important than the foundation. The function

In what ways is your church like an extended family? What benefits do you get from it? What do you bring to it that solidifies and enriches the family?

of the cornerstone is signified by the verb "fitted together" (see 2:21). It embraces the complicated process
of masonry by which stones are fitted together and
aligned, which is what Christ is doing in building His
church.

Paul referred to the "whole building" (2:21), which
can mean all of the building that is being accomplished.
The description of a building under construction is indicated by the word "growing" (2:21). It conveys the
idea of a dynamic church in the process of growth.
Paul again picked up temple imagery and applied it to
the church. The true temple is the whole church.

The major theme of union with Christ reappears in
Paul's conclusion to this section (v. 22). He described
the purpose of the process as the people of God becoming "a dwelling of God in the Spirit." It denotes the divine resting place or habitation. Paul declared that
God's abode is not in the Jerusalem temple but in the
church. This is accomplished by the work of the Spirit
who indwells the new believing community.

Church growth involves numerical growth and the spiritual nurture and development of members. A church under construction continues to reach people and to disciple them. We cannot afford to fall into the trap of "either-or"; growth must be "both-and."

[1]See R. Kent Hughes, *Ephesians: The Mystery of the Body of Christ* (Wheaton:
Crossway Books, 1990), 65.

[2]I have been greatly helped at this point by the insights of John R. W. Stott, *God's
New Society: The Message of Ephesians* (Downers Grove, Ill.: InterVarsity, 1979), 69-85.

[3]F. F. Bruce, *The Epistle to the Ephesians* (Old Tappan: Fleming H. Revell Co.,
1961), 51.

[4]Craig S. Keener, *Bible Background Commentary: New Testament* (Downers Grove,
Ill.: InterVarsity, 1993), 544. See Josephus, *Jewish Antiquities* 15.11.5; and *The Jewish
War*, 5.5.2.

[5]Quoted by Ralph P. Martin, "Ephesians" in *The Broadman Bible Commentary*, vol.
11 (Nashville: Broadman Press, 1971), 146.

[6]See the discussion of options in Andrew T. Lincoln, "Ephesians," vol 42 in *Word
Biblical Commentary* (Dallas: Word, 1990), 142.

Chapter 4

An Amazing Spiritual Mission

Ephesians 3:1-13

A. Revelation of the Divine Mystery (3:1-6)

B. Commission of the Divine Ministry (3:7-10)

C. Agency of the Divine Mission (3:11-13)

Mysteries captivate modern readers and television viewers. Books sold by authors such as John Grisham and regular television programs such as "Murder She Wrote" have been inviting to many of us because of the thrill of mystery. The English word *mystery* involves solving a puzzle or a riddle by determining a series of clues regarding who performed a particular act such as a robbery or a murder. We particularly are impressed with sleuths who can unravel these enigmas. These ideas are accurate associations with the English word *mystery*, but they are misleading in understanding what the word means in Ephesians 3.

In the New Testament, the Greek term *musterion* [moose TAY ree on] means "something that is beyond natural knowledge but has been opened to us by divine revelation through the Holy Spirit." Ephesians has been called the "epistle of the mystery."[1] Paul used the term six times in this letter. In Ephesians he presented the most detailed New Testament exposition of this concept. Paul's spiritual mission was made manifest as a divine mystery.

48

Revelation of the Divine Mystery (3:1-6)

Paul again began a prayer for his readers as he did in the opening chapter (1:15-23). However, he quickly was interrupted again with another thought as the Holy Spirit moved him, leading him to another idea. The mention of the Gentiles reminded Paul that God not only saved them by His grace and reconciled them to one another by Jesus' sacrificial death (2:1-22). God also had united them on an equal basis in the church. God had not revealed this aspect of His eternal plan in times past, but He had made it known through Paul's ministry and proclamation. Under the Spirit's inspiration, Paul called his ministry and proclamation a "mystery."

> Why is every member of equal importance in the church? How can you help implement this awareness?

Paul's Present Circumstances (3:1)

Before Paul launched into his discussion of the divine mystery's being revealed, he further described his present circumstances. In 3:1, he used the phrase "for this reason," but he left his thought unfinished until 3:14. The thought of his imprisonment and his special calling to the Gentiles reminded him that he was in prison because he had obeyed Christ (see Acts 21:27—22:29; 28:16-30).

As an apostle—one sent by Christ's authority—Paul's ministry was not self-generated but ordained by God. Thus, he could not keep from preaching Jesus Christ. He recognized that he was to be a clay jar that carried the treasure of the gospel (see 2 Cor. 4:7). Paul's words in 3:1 celebrated his present circumstances in light of God's will and calling for his life. So, writing from prison, Paul's song and his words went forth. Other important Christian writings have come from prison, such as Saint John of the Cross from his Toledo cell and John Bunyan from the Bedford jail. Even though the circumstances were different, Dietrich Bonhoeffer and Charles Colson wrote from 20th-century prisons. Even

> Paul is an excellent example of a believer who allowed God to make his difficult situation redemptive. Instead of wallowing in self-pity, Paul used his imprisonment to minister to others. How can we let God use our difficulties to help others?

in prison, Paul's thoughts turned to his mission, ministry, and message that summarized his apostolic calling.

Paul's Stewardship of Grace (3:2-5)

The phrase "if indeed you have heard" (v. 2) perhaps indicates that the Letter to the Ephesians was intended for a broader audience than merely the Ephesian church (see comment on 1:1). The Ephesian church would have known of Paul's special calling firsthand.

The phrase "stewardship of God's grace" refers to Paul's unique ministry and is not presumptive. His words describe the implementation of a divine strategy. We should understand Paul's reference to "grace" as the equipping grace that enabled him to serve as a missionary. It also included the idea of extending the gospel privileges to the Gentiles (see Acts 11:20-23). Notice that Paul maintained such grace was given to him for the Gentiles' benefit.

How does God equip us to perform the tasks to which He has called us? What resources does your church provide to help you fulfill your ministry tasks?

The administration of grace had to do with the mystery. As mentioned previously, a mystery points to something that once was hidden or secret and now has been revealed through means impossible by human discovery. The mystery revealed is that God determined to incorporate the Gentiles into the one body of the church as equal partners with Israel (3:6).[2] Paul's purpose was not to announce the conversion of Jews and certainly not to proclaim the Judaizing of Gentiles. His purpose was to celebrate the new race—the new family of God, the church. God's active plan is being worked out dynamically and is being revealed step-by-step. This work continues through the church's missionary enterprise as generation after gen-

In what ways can we celebrate God's new family, the church? Why are times of celebration important for a church?

eration, group after group, have responded to the gospel throughout the ages.

The concept of mystery played a significant role in Paul's thought. In Ephesians 1:9, "mystery" refers to God's plan to unite in Christ all things in heaven and on earth (1:10). This refers to subduing everything, especially hostile powers, under Christ's lordship (see 1:22-23). Christ will bring all things to their providential destiny by providing ultimate redemption for believers and by overcoming the opposing forces. The focus of the mystery that God revealed to Paul on the Damascus Road was Christ Himself, for in Him the unseen God is made known fully. As a steward of the mystery, Paul understood that the Gentiles were destined to be fellow heirs, members of the same body and partakers of the same promises as the Jews (3:6). God's reconciling Jews and Gentiles in one body revealed God's manifold wisdom for Paul's readers to see. The church's existence bears witness to the "stewardship" (3:2) of the mystery that points to the defeat and the overthrow of the hostile powers.

The mystery revealed in Paul's Letter to the Ephesians was not to be confused with pagan mysteries. Christ's bringing "all things" under His rule implied the ultimate doom of the false deities invoked in the magic and in mystery religions. Christ is the beginning point for a true understanding of the concept of mystery in Ephesians as is true in Paul's other writings. A number of mysteries with unique meanings do not exist. One supreme mystery exists, and it has a number of applications. In 3:1-13, the application of the mystery is focused on the church.[3]

Ultimately, as observed in 1:9-10; 2:11-22, the unveiled mystery is that God had terminated Israel's theocracy. He had replaced it with a new international

> Sometimes we almost automatically think of stewardship in terms of money. We may expand the boundaries to include time and talents. Stewardship involves all of life—work, leisure, intellect, influence, love, compassion. We cannot frame an exhaustive list. We are stewards, period.

> What implications does the church's being an international community have for the inclusion and the affirmation of ethnics in our churches? How can we reach out to other ethnic groups?

community—the church, the body of Christ that is united with Him. All believers are now on equal terms without distinction (see Gal. 3:28; 1 Cor. 12:13).

God had not revealed the mystery fully to anyone until He gave it to the church through the apostles and the prophets (3:5).[4] Although Paul was a recipient of this revelation (3:3), no doubt the other apostles also were recipients.

Gentiles as Equal Participants in the Plan of Redemption (3:6)

The importance of the threefold use of the word "fellow" indicates what is at the heart of the mystery. The Gentiles are "fellow heirs," "fellow members of the body," and "fellow partakers of the promise in Christ Jesus through the gospel." These key phrases show that believers in Christ are co-inheritors of God's kingdom.

The phrases also characterize the new community of believers that was to exist with Christ as its Head. The union of Jews and Gentiles into one body was astounding to first-century observers.

However, it is a logical consequence of the gospel truth that God accepts all persons who believe. The union shows the equality and the fellowship that Gentiles have with Jews in the church. The Gentiles would turn to God and be saved as the Old Testament prophesied (see Isa. 42:1-9; 56:6-8). That the Gentiles would have equal footing with God's covenant people was the new aspect of God's revelation.

> In what ways have you seen others signal that some church members are insignificant? In the margin list actions you will take to oppose that and to affirm all members of your church.

Commission of the Divine Ministry (3:7-10)

> To those who see themselves as ministers for Christ, no task is too small or inconsequential.

Paul was enlisted in the service of the gospel, not through his own ambition but as a result of God's calling. He was called as a "minister" (*diakonos* [dee AH ki noss], v. 7), meaning "one who serves tables and is always at the master's bidding." The term denotes a per-

52

son who lives and works in Christ's service in the church. Paul knew that his response to Christ's calling came about only by God's power and grace. The traumatic transformation that changed him from an enemy of the cross into a friend of the gospel was an act of divine grace and power, which are now at work in the church (see 1:19-20).

Personal Insight (3:7-8)

Paul claimed that he was "the very least of all saints" (3:8). Literally, Paul wrote that he was "more leaster"—a combination of a superlative and a comparative in one Greek term. The unusual word may have been a playful allusion to his name. Formerly he was "Saul" of the tribe of Benjamin, considered the smallest tribe according to tradition; his Greek name was "Paul," which in Latin means "little." Paul really acknowledged that in himself he was a nobody; but in Christ, God made him a somebody. This kind of recognition leads to the humility required to be Christ's effective servant in the church. What Paul did as a servant was to preach the riches and unsearchable judgments of the kingdom (see Rom. 11:33). The emphasis is on the boundless treasury of riches in Christ, a wealth whose limit no one ever can find. The treasury is far beyond what we can know but not beyond what we can appreciate—at least in part. Again we see the importance of Paul's earlier prayer for the eyes of our heart to be enlightened so that we can understand these marvelous truths.

> Is humility defined in terms of consistently putting ourselves down, or is it an honest assessment of who we are and what we can do with Christ's help? Explain.

> What treasures have you discovered in your relationship with Christ?

Personal Privilege (3:9-10)

Paul's privileged position was to make plain God's plan, to shine a searchlight so that no one would be in the dark. His task was to bring to light what previously had been hidden. This mystery, now available to all people, was concealed in God's mind (3:9) and not even revealed to angels. God brought the world into being with this strategy in place (see 1:9-10), but in divine wisdom God chose to make known His plan in the stage-by-stage or step-by-step manner. This helps us see that the church is not an afterthought in God's plan of salvation for the ages. The church is now the instrument that proclaims this divine message.

God's intent was that through the church, the "manifold wisdom of God" should be made known (3:10). The term "manifold" means "multicolored or multifaceted like a beautiful jewel." The history of the Christian church and the unfolding drama of redemption is a graduate school for the rulers and authorities in the heavenly realms. To the degree the church carries out God's plan, it displays God's wisdom to angels and to spiritual powers in heaven.

> The church is to give to the world a clear witness of God's love, mercy, and grace. A loving, witnessing, ministering fellowship sends a needed message to needy people.

Agency of the Divine Mission (3:11-13)

The church is central to God's working in history. History is not a series of random events, a cyclical process, or a process of opposites clashing and merging into concepts that cannot be understood. History is HIS story moving in a providential direction. God is Lord over history. John R. Stott wrote that not only is the church central to history but also to the gospel and to Christian living. The gospel is good news of a new society and of a new life.[5] The gospel is more than good news for me; it is good news for us, for the community of faith. Paul wanted his readers to understand the gospel beyond individualistic terms and to move toward a corporate and a community understanding. The church is central to our living out our faith commitment. We cannot push to the edge what is central for God. Thus, as members of

> How can we help fellow Christians live out their faith commitment? In the margin, write the name of another believer whom you will seek to encourage and to assist.

54

the church we approach God with freedom and confidence and receive encouragement for the pilgrimage.

The Church as Divine Agent

The church is the community of people who have accepted God's offer of salvation. The church provides order, organization, and mission directives for God's people. As far as humanly possible, all believers in Christ are to be involved in Christ's visible, organized church; and every person in the church is to be related rightly to Christ by faith. Paul's writings, more than any other writings in the New Testament, help us understand the church's significance. In Ephesians, Paul moved beyond an understanding of the church as a local body of believers to include the people of God on earth at any one time, plus all believers in heaven and on earth. This is the true, invisible, universal church.

At Pentecost, God inaugurated the church as His new society (Acts 2). He founded it on Christ's finished work (Acts 2:22-24) and the Holy Spirit's baptizing work (1 Cor. 12:13). The church is a mystery (Eph. 3:1-6) that Christ prophesied (Matt. 16:18) and that was revealed at the Spirit's coming at Pentecost. The church has Christ's apostles and prophets as its foundation and Christ as the cornerstone (Eph. 2:20-21).

The Church as a Divine Fellowship

Understanding what the believing community is precedes an understanding of what it does. In origin and in purpose, the church is God's church. We do not create the church by our efforts, but we receive it as God's gift. It is constituted by Him and for Him. Membership is by divine initiative; God creates a fellowship of people indwelt by the Holy Spirit, a community of believers whom God has called as saints. The New Testament presents the church as the household of faith (Gal. 6:10), the fellowship of the Spirit (Phil. 2:1), the household of God and the pillar of truth (1 Tim. 3:15), and the bride of Christ (Rev. 19:7). In Ephesians, Paul por-

Fellowship is more than being friendly and socializing. Christian fellowship is sharing life's ups and downs, good and bad, in genuine concern. It is sharing in Christ's work, shouldering loads and helping others with their loads where possible. Christian fellowship is being partners in life's greatest enterprise.

55

trayed the church as the body of Christ (1:22-23), the new creation (2:15), and the building or temple of the Holy Spirit (2:21).

The church reflects many images. The idea of the church as God's people pictures its universality—that is, believers who cross all segments of society (Gal. 3:28). The image of the new creation pictures Christ's victory over evil as a new humanity in the midst of the old. The household of God points to the visible form of God's people who relate to one another in community and who constitute the new creation. The body of Christ shows Christ's presence in the world, though people experience and know it mystically. The church is more than human organization; it is a visible and a tangible expression of the people who are reconciled to Christ and to one another.

Would you describe the church as an organization or as an organism? Explain.

The Church's Divine Mandate

Joining with the church's confession throughout the ages, we can maintain that the church is one, holy, universal, and apostolic. The emphasis in Paul's Letter to the Ephesians is on the church's oneness (see 4:1-6). However, the other truths are important in order for us to understand a full picture of the church. Because of the apostles' important role, the church must remain in continuity with the past and must maintain the apostolic doctrine and practice made known to us in the Holy Scriptures (see Eph. 2:20; 3:2-13). The church's mission is fivefold: worship, fellowship, ministry, evangelism, and discipleship.[6] Ultimately, the church must proclaim Christ's work to a lost and dying world.

In which aspects of the church's mission is your church doing well? Which areas need to be strengthened? What can you do to strengthen one area?

For the church's worship, praise, and prayer to be authentic its fellowship must be caring, its outreach must be compassionate, and its teaching must be informative and edifying. The church's members must pray, work, and even suffer (Eph. 3:13) together.

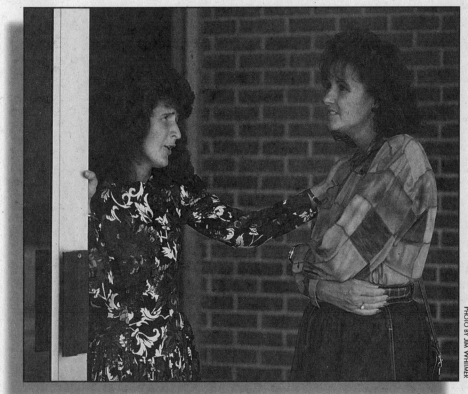

Photo by Jim Whitmer

Church members help their church fulfill its mission as they reach out to the hurting.

[1]P. T. O'Brien, "Mystery," *Dictionary of Paul and His Letters* (Downers Grove, Ill.: InterVarsity, 1993), 621-23.

[2]F. F. Bruce, *The Epistles to the Colossians, to Philemon, and to the Ephesians* (Grand Rapids: Wm. B. Eerdmans Publishing Co., 1984), 315-17.

[3]O'Brien, 621-23; and Charles C. Ryrie, "The Mystery in Ephesians 3," *Bibliotheca Sacra* 123 (1966): 24-31.

[4]See Seyoon Kim, *The Origin of Paul's Gospel* (Grand Rapids: Wm. B. Eerdmans Publishing Co., 1982), 21-25.

[5]See John R. W. Stott, *God's New Society: The Message of Ephesians* (Downers Grove, Ill.: InterVarsity Press, 1979), 127-29.

[6]See the five aspects discussed in Gene Mims, *Kingdom Principles for Church Growth* (Nashville: Convention Press, 1994), 33-66; and James T. Draper, Jr., *Bridges to the Future: A Challenge to Southern Baptists* (Nashville: Convention Press, 1994), 45-49.

Chapter 5

A Prayer for Love and Power

Ephesians 3:14-21

A. Approach to Prayer (3:14-15)
B. Desire for the Saints (3:16-19)
C. Assurance of God's Abilities (3:20)
D. Ascription of God's Glory (3:21)

Life places heavy demands on most of us. Difficulties invade our lives, bringing fear, pain, anxiety, stress, and loss. Only in Christ can we find the spiritual resources to cope with crises.

Perhaps you have heard about a man chatting with a salesperson. They stood in the beautiful showroom where yachts and cabin cruisers glittered with elegance. The salesperson told the customer that if he had to ask how much the boats cost, they were too expensive for him. No believer ever has to worry about having inadequate spiritual resources to meet life's demands. Ephesians 3:14-21 is an important section that has the second of two prayers in the letter. The first prayer emphasized the need for spiritual enlightenment (1:15-23). The prayer in 3:14-21 emphasized enabling. Being enabled to meet life's demands is not as much a matter of knowing as of being. Paul's prayer was for believers to know what God had for them and by faith to make it a vital part of their lives.

Approach to Prayer (3:14-15)

In verse 14, Paul resumed the prayer that he began in 3:1 and that he interrupted temporarily. In this prayer, he asked that the readers might be blessed with inner strength, with insightful understanding, and with spiritual excellence. Paul's prayers are God's promises. We are justified in taking these lofty petitions as being distinct decla-

58

rations of God's desire for us. In this beautiful prayer, we find a great confidence in God and a boldness in approaching Him that can challenge us to a more fruitful prayer life.

How would you define prayer? What part does prayer play in your daily life?

A focus on Paul's approach to prayer is also a window through which we can understand the importance of prayer in the early church. These Christians viewed prayer as the means by which God's guidance and power came to the church. The first Christians prayed in many circumstances:

1. while they awaited the fulfillment of Jesus' promise concerning the Holy Spirit's coming and the birth of the church (Acts 1:14);

2. when enemies threatened them or when they suffered (Acts 4:23-31; 12:12; 16:25);

3. when they were confronted by others' sickness or death (Acts 9:40; 28:8);

4. when they were concerned about others' spiritual needs (Acts 8:15);

5. when they left fellow believers (Acts 20:36-38; 21:5);

6. when they selected or commissioned persons for special service (Acts 1:24; 6:6; 13:2-3; 14:23);

7. when they faced martyrdom at the hands of persecutors (Acts 7:59-60).[1]

We may not understand the reason some things happen to us, and the outcome may be uncertain. We can be sure that God loves us and is present with us.

In the early church, believers prayed at set times and places (Acts 3:1); in homes (1:13-14); in the temple (2:46-47; 3:1); on the seashore (21:5); aboard ship (27:35); and in jail (16:25). In Ephesians, Paul prayed because he was concerned about his readers' spiritual needs even while he was in a Roman prison cell.

How does praying for others help us cope with our own difficulties?

Confidence in God's Ability (3:14)

Paul expressed a prayer that grew out of his awareness of all that God does in believers. Bishop Handley Moule wrote: "Who has not read and re-read the closing verses of the third chapter of the Ephesians with the feeling of one permitted to look through parted cur-

PHOTO BY JIM WHITMER

To pray as Paul did for the Ephesians is to express great confidence in God.

tains into the Holiest Place of the Christian life?"[2]

Verses 14-15 express urgency. Paul knelt before God. Standing was a common posture in prayer (see Luke 18:11-13). Sitting, prostrating oneself, (see Matt. 26:39), or even walking were permissible. However, to kneel indicated a sense of urgency, which Jesus did in Gethsemane (see Luke 22:41).

Confidence in God's Care (3:15)

The phrase "from whom every family in heaven and on earth derives its name" heightens the sense of God's power. This phrase is a basic affirmation of God as Creator of all species of living beings, as the One who gives meaning, shape, and purpose to each individual.[3]

Paul identified God as Father (Eph. 3:14) by virtue of His creative work and His providing redemption for believers. Fatherhood is God's, and we should not understand it in terms of human relationships. It describes God as One to whom we can commit our lives and our prayers in confidence.

If we understood God as some impersonal force, then we could not address Him as Father. Paul, following Jesus' words (see Matt. 6:9-10), did not refer to an impersonal "unmoved mover" or "ground of being." Instead, he addressed God as Father. When we recognize God as our loving Heavenly Father, we can approach Him in genuine humility, confidence, and devotion. When we can address God as Father, we can bring to Him our deepest concerns and our loftiest praise. God as Father is accessible, personal, and caring as opposed to an impersonal force. That He is our Father points to His majestic greatness and to His sovereignty.

Desire for the Saints (3:16-19)

The source for Paul's lofty petitions was God's glorious riches. In 3:16-19, Paul prayed for believers to be (1) "strengthened," (2) "rooted and grounded," and (3) "filled" via the work of the three Persons of the Trinity: Spirit, Christ, and God.

Strengthened by the Spirit's Power (3:16)

First Paul prayed for inner power; that is, power through the Holy Spirit in the inner being. This power is not of ourselves; God grants it. This kind of power is the result of Christ's dwelling in our hearts (v. 17). The Greek word for "dwell" used in verse 17 means "to reside permanently, to be completely at home." The prayer indicates that the Holy Spirit will not merely be present in our lives, but He will be resident and preeminent. Thus, believers can be strengthened continually and intensely, not merely helped occasionally.

Grounded in the Love of Christ (3:17-19a)

Using a combination of agricultural and architectural illustrations, Paul prayed that his readers would be "rooted and grounded in love" along with all believers (3:17-18). Notice that this rooting and grounding takes place within the context of the church. Again, in this passage Paul emphasized the corporate nature of the Christian life in the church. He

How would you describe Christ's love? In the margin, write three expressions of Christ's love that you have experienced.

61

did not write of individualistic Christianity but of his concern for individuals within the context of a believing, cooperating community. He wanted believers to grasp the greatness of Christ's love.

Paul prayed that believers could understand how wide, long, high, and deep is Christ's great love for His people. His love is as wide as all humanity and bridges the gap between all cultural and ethnic divisions, including that of Jews and Gentiles. Christ's love is as long as all eternity. It is completely sufficient and inexhaustible. It is as high as the heavens and as deep as our darkest sin. At the cross of Christ, God's love reconciles the height of heaven and the lowest sinner. Jesus' life and death exemplified divine love by His making the ultimate sacrifice. This most valuable redemption delivered sinners from enslavement. It reconciled and restored sinners from estrangement to full fellowship and inheritance in the household of God.[4]

Christ's infinite compassion moved Him to make His great self-sacrifice. Beyond the four dimensions of width, length, height, and depth, Paul prayed that believers would grasp the greatness of Christ's love even to a fifth dimension. He stated that it is unmeasurable. This does not mean that it is unknowable. It means that Christ's love is so great it cannot be known completely. To paraphrase the hymn writer, the love of God is far greater than pen or tongue can tell. It reaches to the highest star and even to the depth of our sinful hell. Paul wanted his readers to understand the greatness of Christ's love that empowers us in our Christian living.

What are some valid requests we can make of God in prayer? What are some improper requests?

Filled by the Greatness of God (3:19b)

Third, Paul wanted believers to be filled to the measure of the fullness of God with all of God's energies and powers. We can draw on and trust in God's infiniteness. Paul's prayer reminds us of Jesus' words in John 7:37-39 inviting people to come to Him and to drink with the result that the Spirit would fill them. We can drink of this water and never thirst.

Parents can teach their children to pray by praying with them.

Paul made three requests in his prayer in Ephesians 3:16-19. However, we must not look on them as isolated, individual petitions. These requests are more like diverse aspects of a portrait observed from different angles. One request leads into the next, and so on. Paul prayed that the inner person have spiritual strength that will, in turn, lead to a deeper experience with Christ. This deeper experience will enable us to take hold of Christ's great love, which will result in our being "filled up to all the fulness of

63

God" (3:19). Paul prayed for apprehension of God's strength, depth, and fullness. In one sense, believers already have obtained these lofty petitions because we have been made full in Christ (see Col. 2:9-10). In our standing before Christ, we are complete in Him; but practically we enjoy these spiritual graces only to the degree that we apprehend them by faith. The resources are ours. Paul prayed that believers would accept them, enjoy them, and use them to understand what being a part of the community of faith in service to Christ means.

> What are evidences that a person has inner spiritual strength? How does a believer gain such strength?

Assurance of God's Abilities (3:20)

After considering the marvelous spiritual truths in 3:16-19, Paul burst into a grand doxology concerning God's abilities. The prayer was to God the Father with assurance of the indwelling strength of God the Spirit who is made accessible to us through God the Son.

Assured of God's abilities, Paul built on the assurance step-by-step proclaiming that:

1. God is able.
2. He is able to do all that we ask.
3. He is able to do all that we think.
4. He is able to do all that we ask or think.
5. He is able to do exceedingly abundantly beyond all that we can ask or think.
6. He "is able to do exceeding abundantly beyond all that we ask or think, according to the power that works within us."

> Often, God chooses to work through caring, responsive people. When we are available for God's use, we can make His compassion and grace believable and attractive to people who need His love.

Incredibly, God can do immeasurably more than we can think or ask. He is able to do so, for He is neither an idle nor an inactive God. He is able to do what we ask because He loves us, and He cares for us. He hears us because He is our Father. He is able to do what we think, because in His infinite wisdom He knows our thoughts even before we think them. He is able to do all things because of His great power that never runs out of energy. He is able to do more than all we ask or think, for His expectations are higher than ours. He is able to do exceeding abundantly beyond all that we ask or think, for He does not give His grace in insufficient measure. He is able to do vastly more because He is the infinite God of super abundance and immeasurable grace.[5]

God is able to do whatever He wills and to do it the way He wills. Yet, He never chooses to do anything contrary to His nature. He generally works through obedient people of faith, but He also can work through people who disobey Him. His eternal purposes will not be frustrated (see Eph. 1:11). We can petition our loving, gracious, infinite, and all-powerful God to hear and to answer our prayers. Paul's confidence in God's ability represents a boldness that we also must claim.

> God can do far more than we ask or think. Why do you think He sometimes chooses not to act as we have asked or to give what we feel we need?

Ascription of God's Glory (3:21)

The ultimate goal of our existence is God's glory. Paul prayed that God's glory would be manifested in the church and in Christ, in the bride and in the bridegroom, in the community of peace and in the Peacemaker, in history and in eternity. God has called the church to an extraordinary position that exceeds our capacity for imagining. In the eternal state, the church will keep on expanding in its capacity to bring glory to God for all eternity.

As we conclude our study of the first major section of Ephesians (1:1—3:21), we can echo Paul's concluding "Amen" (3:21). We have learned that we need to be praying three things for one another even as Paul prayed for his readers. We can pray for inner strength in order to be empowered to understand and to do what God has for us to do. We can pray for love so that our lives will be rooted and grounded in God's boundless compassion. We can pray for ever-growing fullness in our ongoing relationship with God.

Paul's prayer is God's revealed will for His people. Like Paul, we must reclaim the activity of great praying in the church. The focus of attention in our prayers should be our inner being; we should pray for the transformation of

Identify elements of genuine worship. What elements do you need to strengthen?

our character so that we will be more like Christ. We must recognize that the church is to glorify God, and we must worship Him. What a privilege is ours to share in an able God's redemptive plan and to worship Him in spirit and in truth (see John 4:24)!

[1]See Stanley J. Grenz, *Prayer: The Cry for the Kingdom* (Peabody, Mass.: Hendrickson Publishers, 1988).

[2]Handley C. G. Moule, *Veni Creator: Thoughts on the Person and Work of the Holy Spirit of Promise* (London: Hodder and Stoughton, pref. 1890), 228.

[3]Max Turner, "Ephesians," in *New Bible Commentary: 21st Century Edition*, ed. D. A. Carson and others (Downers Grove, Ill.: InterVarsity Press, 1994), 1235.

[4]Though we must be careful with such "spiritualized interpretation," we can nevertheless be motivated to healthy meditation on the greatness of God's love for us. This tradition is rich throughout the church since the time of Augustine. See Charles Spurgeon, "Heavenly Geometry" in *The Metropolitan Tabernacle Pulpit*, vol. 12 (Pasadena, Tex.: Pilgrim Publications, reprint 1980), 469-80.

[5]See A. W. Tozer, *The Knowledge of the Holy* (New York: Harper & Brothers, 1961); also J. I. Packer, *Knowing God* (Downers Grove, Ill.: InterVarsity Press, 1973).

Chapter 6

A Portrait of the Church

Ephesians 4:1-16

A. Unity of the Church (4:1-6)
B. Variety in the Church (4:7-12)
C. Goal of the Church (4:13-16)

What is the glue that holds a diverse group of people together? For a team in sports, the cohesive factor is a common goal: to win—a game, a championship, a trophy. For people combatting drunken drivers or violence in a city or a neighborhood, the commonality often is children's tragic deaths that have moved parents to unified action. For people championing the cause of the homeless, the physically or mentally challenged, the helpless, the unifying factor is compassion. For proponents of a political candidate, the unifying force is electing a person who may make a positive contribution to a city, state, or nation. For hobbyists, the bond is a common interest. Diverse people can and do work together in a wide variety of areas, unified around a common objective or concern.

> What factors contribute to your church's unity? to its disunity? What one action will you take to promote unity?

67

What common bonds do believers share? The reader of Ephesians 4:1-16 is struck by Paul's repetition of the word *one*, which occurs seven times. Further observation reveals that the seven "ones" are grounded in the three members of the Trinity ("one Spirit," 4:4; "one Lord," 4:5; and "one God and Father of all," 4:6). Look at Paul's seven "ones" and our corporate Christian experience.

Unity of the Church (4:1-6)

Ephesians 4 begins a series of exhortations for the new community of believers. In chapters 1—3, Paul brilliantly disclosed for his readers God's eternal purpose as it is being worked out in history. Paul indicated that God is creating something entirely new—a new life for individuals, yes; but more than that He is creating a new people, the church. This magnificent vision portrays the reconciliation of an alienated and fractured humanity.

Worthy Living (4:1-2)

The reconciled new humanity has new standards. Paul urged his readers, "Live a life worthy of the calling you have received" (NIV).[1] The exhortation serves as a major transition in the letter as it moves from the church's credenda (belief statement) to the church's agenda (mission statement). Paul insisted that the believers' behavior was to be worthy of their divine calling.

Correct belief is important; sound doctrine is essential. However, belief must issue in exemplary behavior; theology must be translated into a healthy lifestyle. Our behavior can confirm or refute what we profess to believe.

Verse 2 presents five virtues that characterize and exemplify life worthy of the Christian calling. The first virtue, "humility," points to our ultimate dependence on God. People in the ancient world despised humility. Seldom if ever did they admire or approve of the quality. Unique to Christianity is the model of humility that Jesus gave. He humbled Himself, even to the point of dying on a cross (see Phil. 2:5-8). Humility is an absolute necessity to unity, because pride stands behind most discord.

"Gentleness," the second virtue Paul mentioned, suggests strength under control. Some versions translate this term as "meekness." The idea should not be associated with weakness. Rather, it is a work of divine grace in believers that produces patience, quiet restraint, and submission to God. This characteristic is particularly necessary for church leaders who should exercise their leadership in a spirit of gentleness. Humility and gentleness were evident in Christ, who described Himself as "gentle and humble in heart" (Matt. 11:29).

The third virtue is "patience" (Eph. 4:2). Patience is the disposition of a person who is "slow to anger" (Jas. 1:19). Patient people demonstrate long-suffering in dealing with insulting and aggravating people, as God in Christ acts toward us (see Rom. 2:4). The next quality, "forbearance," further explains patience. Forbearance expresses a mutual tolerance without which no group of people can live together in peace.[2]

"Love" is the final quality that embraces the previous four. Paul grounded the four characteristics "in love" (Eph. 4:2).[3] In Ephesians 3:17, he prayed for believers to be "rooted and grounded in love." If the church is to demonstrate unity before a watching world, love—as the embracing virtue and the crown of all virtues— must characterize God's people (see John 13:34-35). God's people will have genuine unity only when these Christian virtues characterize our lives individually and corporately.

Which of the five virtues Paul listed—humility, gentleness, patience, forbearance, and love—do you need to strengthen? Choose one that you will cooperate with God in developing.

Spirit-Energized Unity (4:3)

Believers are to walk or to live in a way worthy of their calling, which Paul described in Ephesians 1—3. Some Bible students have outlined the three major sections of the book as sit (2:6), walk (4:1), and stand (6:11). Perhaps a better outline is worship, walk and witness, and warfare. In the introductory section on walking and witnessing, 4:1-3, Paul called for believers to make their business bringing about unity in the body of Christ. We are not to take a wait-and-see attitude, but we are to be eager to do what we can "to preserve the unity of the Spirit in the bond of peace" (4:3).

The unity of which Paul wrote in verse 3 is the unity of heart that God's Spirit energizes in a community of believers and is made visible to an observing world. Ephesians 4:1-3 parallels Paul's command to the Philippian Christians (Phil. 2:2-5).

The relationship between Ephesians 4:2 and 4:3 is clear. When believers cultivate and practice the virtues described in 4:2, they display and preserve the unity of the Spirit. Paul's stirring challenge in verse 3 often falls on deaf ears. God is the Author of peace, and stirring up dissension among His people is detestable to Him (see Prov. 6:16-19). From his admonition to unity, Paul moved to the basis of this unity.

Is peace in a church the absence of disagreement and even conflict, or is it an atmosphere in which people are encouraged to express diverse views in an attempt to see and to do God's will? Explain.

In Ephesians 4:4-6 are the seven "ones" that constitute the foundation on which the God in three Persons (the Trinity) creates a true oneness in the church. We will view Paul's plan from the vantage point of the work of the one Spirit (creating one body), the one Lord Jesus Christ (creating one hope, faith, and baptism), and the one God the Father (bringing about the one people of God).

One Body (4:4a)

First, "one body" exists because only "one Spirit" exists. "One body" refers to the church, the body of Christ (Eph. 1:23; 2:16). It is comprised of Jews and Gentiles, free people and slaves, and males and females (1 Cor. 12:13; Gal. 3:28). Cohesion of the body comes from the Holy Spirit who indwells, seals, and energizes it (1:13; 4:30). As the body is one though its members are many, so the Spirit is one though His gifts and His operations are many (see 4:7-12).

One Hope, Faith, and Baptism (4:4b-5)

Second, "one hope," "one faith," and "one baptism" exist because only one Lord exists. As the great hymn of the faith proclaims:

The church's one foundation
Is Jesus Christ her Lord;
She is His new creation;
By Spirit and the Word:
From heav'n He came and sought her
To be His holy bride,
With His own blood He bought her,
And for her life He died.[4]

Jesus Christ is the One in whom we have believed, into whom the Spirit has baptized us, and for whose coming we wait with expectant hope.

The "one hope" (4:4) of our calling is the hope of sharing Christ's glory. This one hope is set before all believers, and no distinction exists between them. The believing community has no favored members for whom better things are reserved.

The "one faith" (4:5) may denote the act of believing, or it may refer to the substance of a person's belief. The phrase is true in both senses. No Christian unity is possible unless believers share a common commitment to Christian doctrine ("the faith which was once for all delivered to the saints," Jude 3). But the emphasis of Ephesians 4:5 is the believers' shared experience of faith in Christ and the same access to Him.

"One baptism" (4:5) pictures the outward expression of the person exercising faith in the one Lord. Baptism is the visible sign in water by which persons who believe the gospel, repent of their sins, and publicly acknowl-

> The rich diversity in a church helps it function smoothly. Each member brings something unique and necessary to the body. Combining the spiritual gifts allows a church to reach people for Christ and to nurture believers.

> What are the bedrock, non-negotiable elements of your faith? List these in the margin.

71

edge Jesus as Savior and Lord show they are a part of the body of Christ. Both Jewish and Gentile believers acknowledged Jesus as the "one Lord," shared a common faith in Him, and were initiated into Christ and His church in the waters of baptism (see Gal. 3:27).

One People of God (4:6)

The last emphasis of Ephesians 4:1-6 concerning the new humanity is that the one Christian family belongs to the "one God and Father of all who is over all and through all and in all." The previous chapters of Ephesians help us understand that the "all" for whom God is Father are God's people, His redeemed children (see Eph. 1:2,17; 2:18-19; 3:14-15). Unity is imperative because only one Christian faith, hope, baptism, and body exist. This confession rests on the truth that one God exists: Father, Son, and Holy Spirit.[5]

The infighting and the discord that sometimes characterize the church indicate how far we fall short of God's expectations. Genuine commitment on the part of God's people to the Holy Scriptures' authority calls for us to live as the Scriptures instruct us to live. The call for unity among God's people takes high priority in the Scriptures (see Ps. 133:1; John 17:21; 1 Cor. 12:4-13; Eph. 4:1-6). We must confess our sins of disunity and ask God to renew His people. The larger context of Ephesians 4 indicates that Christian unity is expressed through variety (4:7-12) and brings about maturity (4:13-16) and purity (4:17-32) in the church.

If the church truly is to be the people of God, it visibly must exhibit an attitude of unity. God's oneness defines the church's oneness. As God is one in three, so the church is made up of different parts with a variety of expressions; yet the body functions as a unity. Thus, unity in the body of Christ

Why do you think unity in a church is imperative?

What is the difference between unity and uniformity? How can uniformity be detrimental in a church?

72

does not demand uniformity. The church attests to God's oneness (one in three) as it manifests its unity in variety. Let us affirm that the church's visible unity in truth is God's purpose for His people. Likewise, let us pray and work for renewal and unity in our worship, witness, and fellowship. We can petition our Lord to renew the church and to restore its ministries, both to serve and to adore God. We must pray for the Lord to send us power so that His church may be renewed.

Variety in the Church (4:7-12)

Paul moved to discuss the variety within the church's unity. God has granted grace, a portion to each believer, as a gift from Christ. Because each believer has received grace, all believers are on the same level in exercising their grace gifts. The spiritual blessings (1:3) that God graciously has given to all believers at the time of conversion include the distribution of gifted persons (or grace gifts) to the body of Christ.

Gifts to the Church (4:7-10)

In 4:8 Paul alluded to Psalm 68:18. The essence of the psalm is that a military victor has the right to receive gifts from the people he has conquered and who now are his subjects. Paul made a change in his use of the psalm and suggested that Christ has conquered His enemies (Paul being the perfect example) and has given gifts to them. As their Victor, Christ gives gifts to His new devoted followers, His captives.

Ephesians 4:8 is a reference to Christ's ascension and triumphant procession. The verse is not a direct quotation from the Hebrew text of Psalm 68, but it is an allusion to Psalm 68:18. The reference is an example of the way Paul viewed the Scriptures from the perspective of what God had done through Jesus' life, death, and resurrection.[6]

Verses 9-10 are the source of much discussion and difference of opinion. Basically, they indicate that Christ descended to the earth in the incarnation and

In Romans 12:6-8; 1 Corinthians 12:8-11; Ephesians 4:11; 1 Timothy 4:13, Paul listed spiritual gifts God gives His people. No list is exhaustive. God gives many gifts to His people, which they are to use to further His purpose. Every believer has at least one gift.

73

after His resurrection ascended to heaven where He reigns over the church. Some Bible students have interpreted these verses to refer to Christ's descending into hell between His crucifixion and His resurrection. That probably is not the meaning in 4:9 or in 1 Peter 3:18-22. Paul's point was that the resurrected and exalted Christ now imparts all the fullness of His blessings to the church and to the universe (see 1:10,19-23; 3:20-21).[7]

Gifted Leaders in the Church (4:11)

Verse 11 is more about gifted people than about spiritual gifts (as contrasted with 1 Cor. 12—14; Rom. 12). The discussion of gifted people and spiritual gifts is similar in that Christ's gifts to the church are gifted people. Paul mentioned five groups of gifted people: apostles, prophets, evangelists, pastors, and teachers.[8]

Who are gifted people whom God has given your church? How can you affirm, encourage, and support them?

Apostles

Apostles and prophets are foundational for the church's work (see 2:20; 3:5). In 4:11 the word "apostles" does not refer directly to Jesus' twelve disciples. Others named as apostles include James (Gal. 1:19; 1 Cor. 15:7); Barnabas (Acts 14:14); Andronicus and Junias (Rom. 16:7); and perhaps others like Silas, Timothy, Apollos, and certainly Paul. In Ephesians 4:11, the gift of apostleship is distinguished from the office of apostle. The term primarily refers to people sent with a specific divine mission or task. The apostles were the foundation of the church and also functioned as prophets. As "the foundation," they planted churches. They also served as spokesmen for God, bringing new revelation and understanding to the church. All apostles were prophets, but not all prophets were apostles.

Prophets

Prophets provided exhortation, edification, and comfort to the church (see 1 Cor. 14:3). Their responsibility was to reveal God's will to the believers. While all prophets were not apostles, they nevertheless had authority while speaking under the Spirit's inspiration. Prophets spoke by the Spirit's direct illumination, and God's revelation came through prophecy (see 1 Cor. 14:6,26,30-31). Paul made prophetic announcements in Romans 11:25; 1 Corinthians 15:51; and 1 Thessalonians 4:13. Prophets revealed God's will for the present (forthtelling) and predicted the future (foretelling).

Evangelists

Evangelists were gifted to spread the gospel and to plant churches. Apostles also carried out this evangelistic mission. Evangelists proclaimed the good news in word and deed and instructed others in evangelism. Thus, the church could be built up not only in quality but also in quantity through outreach.

Who is to do the work of evangelism? In the margin, list ways to do evangelism.

Most likely, evangelists had mobile ministries, while pastors and teachers functioned in settled congregations. I suggest that prophets and apostles were both local and mobile in their ministries.

Pastors and Teachers

Some Bible students understand "pastors and teachers" to mean one group of people: pastor/teacher. This is grammatically possible, but whether Paul meant one group of people or two is not certain. That he would have envisioned pastors who could not teach or teachers who did not shepherd is highly unlikely.

In what ways can you support and encourage your pastor?

Pastors provided oversight, comfort, and guidance as the church's shepherds (see Acts 20:28; 1 Pet. 5:2-4). Teachers instructed and helped apply God's Word to

75

the life of the church. Teachers were concerned with passing on the church's revealed teachings (see 1 Cor. 15:3-4) rather than bringing new inspirational insights like the prophets. Teachers probably were occupied with instructing new converts and giving ongoing instruction for older believers. The teaching gift is indispensable in building up the church and is necessary to enable believers to distinguish false doctrine from true teaching.

All of the gifts Paul listed are used within the church to encourage, enable, enrich, and enlist people. Encouraging and enabling are necessary to get people moving and working. People need to be motivated for ministry. In addition, the saints must be trained to enable them to carry out the ministries for which they are gifted. Enlistment, the task of both the evangelist and the pastor, is also vitally important to recruit the unchurched people and to lead lost people to Christ. These gifted persons also can be used to enlist other believers into service of the church.

Gifts to Equip for Service (4:12)

God has given gifts or gifted people in order to "prepare God's people for works of service, so that the body of Christ may be built up" (NIV). The purpose of the gifted persons is to equip others to minister. To break Paul's thought at this point is difficult, because like many other long sentences in Ephesians, verses 11-16 form one long sentence in the Greek text.

God still gives gifts to each of us for service in the church, and He graciously gives gifted people for the right place at the right time. Because every member of the church functions within the priesthood of believers, each member worships, offers praise and thanksgiving, and offers his or her own service as a sacrifice to God (see Rom. 12:1-2; Heb. 13:15-16). All believers are to use within the church the gifts given them. God's Spirit has equipped each of us with spiritual gifts for the purpose of ministry.

76

A spiritual gift is a God-given ability for service. The source of the gift is God, and the ability is the means to perform service. The gift is not a place of service, but it is the ability to serve.

God gives the gift. The Spirit empowers its use. Believers help one another develop their gifts for the church's good. We are to be informed as to what the gifts are, to be willing to use our gifts for the church's good, to be active in discovering our gifts, and to be faithful in using them. Verses 13-16 help us understand that exercising our gifts leads the church to unity, stability, and maturity rather than to immaturity, instability, and gullibility.

Just as children help each other develop their skills, so can Christians help other believers develop their spiritual gifts for the church's good.

Goal of the Church (4:13-16)

"All believers are to be involved in ministry, not merely a few select leaders." Do you agree or disagree with that statement? Explain.

The goal of the ministries listed in 4:11-12 is the building up of the church. God gives the gifts in order to equip His people. The Greek word translated "equipping" sometimes was used to refer to mending or restoring people for ministry/service. Verses 11-16 indicate that all believers are to be involved in ministry, not merely a few select leaders. Ministry is to move believers toward accomplishing three goals: (1) unity of faith and the full knowledge of God's Son, (2) maturity, and (3) the fullness of Christ. Obviously, maturity and unity are measured in terms of the relationship of the body to the Head, Christ. Verses 14-16 describe the results of gifted people equipping others for service. When the gifted people equip the church, the community of faith will evidence stability in precept and practice. The church will have transparent relationships where people can speak the truth in love to one another (literally, v. 15 has "truthing in love"). The *Contemporary English Version*[9] (CEV) translates verse 15, "Love should always make us tell the truth. Then we will grow in every way and be more like Christ." Ultimately the church will grow up into Christ "in all aspects" (v. 15), with each part fitting together and supporting the other (v. 16). Christ gives the gifts of ministries, and each member of the body—the church—must function properly if the body is to grow (v. 16). Each member must do the work allotted to him or her. We get our word *harmony* from the Greek term translated "joined . . . together." "Held together" can be translated "fitted together." Each part of the body, in cooperation with the other parts, supplies what he or she is designed to supply. When each member of Christ's body contributes consistently in cooperation with other members, then the body will be built up in love.

We are to have a childlike faith, demonstrating honesty and humility in all things. However, we are not to be childish, which implies a lack of discernment. We are not to be characterized as unstable—whether in family life, personal life, or in the church. People who are unstable often are caught up by trends portrayed in the latest book, conference, or movement. The kind of maturity Paul described in Ephesians 4 leads us away from instability and gullibility. While Christians are to be trusting, they also are to be discerning. We must not presume that everything bearing or using God's name is true. Deliberately designed deceptions offered as counterfeits to the truth are matters about which the church always must remain aware.

> What is the difference between being childlike and being childish? What would you identify as childish behavior in the church?

---

[1]Scripture quotations marked (NIV) are from the Holy Bible, *New International Version*, copyright © 1973, 1978, 1984 by International Bible Society.

[2]See the discussion of these and similar virtues in David S. Dockery, "Fruit of the Spirit," *Dictionary of Paul and His Letters* (Downers Grove, Ill.: InterVarsity Press, 1993), 316-19.

[3]Here I am following the structure suggested by John R. W. Stott, *God's New Society: The Message of Ephesians* (Downers Grove, Ill.: InterVarsity Press, 1979), 148-49.

[4]"The Church's One Foundation," No. 350, *The Baptist Hymnal*, 1991.

[5]Leon Morris, *Expository Reflections on the Letter to the Ephesians* (Grand Rapids: Baker Book House, 1994), 117-20.

[6]See Richard N. Longenecker, *Biblical Exegesis in the Apostolic Period* (Grand Rapids: Wm. B. Eerdmans Publishing Co., 1975); James D. G. Dunn, *Unity and Diversity in the New Testament* (Philadelphia: Westminster Press, 1977), 92.

[7]F. F. Bruce, *The Epistle to the Ephesians* (Old Tappan: Fleming H. Revell Co., 1961), 83-84; D. Edmond Hiebert, *1 Peter* (Chicago: Moody Press, 1992), 239-44.

[8]See Kenneth S. Hemphill, *Spiritual Gifts: Empowering the New Testament Church* (Nashville: Broadman Press, 1988).

[9]Scripture quotations identified as CEV are from the *Contemporary English Version*. Copyright © American Bible Society 1991, 1992. Used by permission.

Chapter 7

Holy Living

Paul's illustration of changing clothes stressed the radical transformation that occurs at conversion. The picture is of a person discarding ragged, dirty clothes for new, clean items. The Christian discards the old person and takes on the new person in Christ.

W e all have heard that clothes do not make the person but they sure help! A book is entitled *Dress for Success*. Manuals on power dressing are available. We have seen advertisements that picture men and women before and after they have put on improved attire. After they are wearing the new suits or dresses, they supposedly are new people. The fashion world promises us a new life through clothing. The problem is that clothing does not make the man or the woman.

In Ephesians 4:17-32, Paul presented a picture of new clothes for the soul, a divine wardrobe that really changes life. The clothing is for the church; it is a heavenly, eternal style that never will go out of fashion. With time, the new wardrobe increases in its fashion and durability. Paul indicated what we need to take off and what we need to put on in order to be dressed properly. If we take his recommendation seriously, we will be dressed for all of life's occasions.

Inward Transformation (4:17-24)

Ephesians 4:17-32 is the practical outworking of 4:1. Believers must abandon the old way of living; they must

80

remove the old clothes and must put on the new, which is putting on Christ. Paul's words to his readers reveal a twofold purpose: (1) to help them understand God's work and the effect of grace on them; and (2) to describe the actions they were to live out that corresponded to the things identified in the first purpose. Before moving in that direction, to see Paul's vivid description of people in rebellion is important.

Former Way of Life (4:17-19)

Paul's exhortation denounced the readers' former way of life. At the same time it denounces the present way of life of people outside the church.[1] Paul contrasted the conduct that should characterize persons who have been taught the Christian tradition to the conduct of people who live according to the world's ways. The content of the exhortation clearly parallels early Christian baptismal practices of putting off old clothes before putting on new clothes to enter the baptismal waters. The picture is amplified by Colossians 3:5-11. However, in the Colossians passage the contrast is between the heavenly and the earthly life; in Ephesians the contrast is between the person's former lifestyle and the new life in Christ.

In Ephesians 4:17-19, Paul strongly insisted that believers were not to fall back into the old patterns of thinking and the resultant behavior that characterized the surrounding Gentile world. Believers were to leave behind an existence in which sin and all of its folly and futility distorted life. Paul wrote that this way of life was characterized by depraved obstinacy, a darkened understanding, death and alienation, and dishonorable passions.

What are essential elements of a distinctively Christian lifestyle? Why is distinguishing between Christians and non-Christians sometimes difficult?

Lifestyle descriptions in ancient Greek and Roman literature shows that Paul was on target in his description of people in rebellion to the truth. In Romans

1:18-32, Paul amplified this description. He declared that unbelievers are stubborn and hard-hearted. He stated that their minds and hearts are ignorant, having been captured by the futility of this world. This shows that not only has sin affected our wills but also our minds.

Paul stated that as a result of the pagan lifestyle, a numbness—a callousness—exists that leads to further degradation. This kind of life is fragmented, aimless, hopeless, and reckless. This recklessness works itself out through dishonorable passions and sensual, selfish greed. Paul declared that these reckless passions had passed the point of feeling and had moved toward total insensitivity. Because of this, a person had no feeling of shame, pain, or sorrow about what he or she was doing. A desire to possess was present, regardless of the means that might be involved. While Paul was describing the ancient Gentile world, obviously his words have many parallels with our world; thus, the Word of God is a fresh Word to us today.[2]

> Why do we become insensitive to sin and more accepting of it? How can we remain sensitive to our sins and the sin around us?

Life in Christ (4:20-21)

Paul moved from the picture of the wrong way of life to what God expects of Christians. Believers who have learned Christ do not and should not live as people who have not learned Christ (v. 20). Paul pictured the truth totally in terms of Christ, who is the Way, the Truth, and the Life (see John 14:6). Christians have learned Christ as subject. They also have learned from Christ as Teacher. Furthermore, they have learned in the sphere of Christ as the realm and the room (school) in which genuine Christian education takes place.[3] Thus, we respond to Jesus not merely as the Savior but as the Lord who has ushered in a rule of righteousness. Christ is light and life, as opposed to the Gentiles' darkened deeds. Paul's readers, as well as contemporary

Micah wrote: "What does the Lord require of you But to do justice, to love kindness, And to walk humbly with your God" (Mic. 6:8). God has revealed what He expects of His people. His expectations are high. Only in His grace and strength can we move toward meeting His demands.

Christians, had heard Christ through the apostles' teachings and writings. Jesus, the perfect Teacher, dealt with each student carefully and individually. Recall the various approaches that He took with Nicodemus (John 3:1-15), the woman at the well (John 4:1-42), and the rich young ruler (Luke 18:18-25). The result of responding to Jesus' teachings is a movement away from corruption and toward a growing likeness of our Savior.

Paul declared that when we put on Christ, we also must shed our former way of life. This clothing illustration indicates that we must walk away from emptiness, darkness, alienation, insensitivity, and recklessness. We must put on the new self with the new mind.[4] These pictures are true for all believers, even though people raised in Christian homes and saved as children often do not experience the ruinous effects of sin to the same degree.

What attitudes, habits, and actions did you have to "put off" when you became a Christian? Which do you have to resist resuming? What new elements have replaced the old?

The renewed person walks with Jesus as Lord as opposed to any other leader. Salvation results in eternal life and escape from the wrath to come. This salvation involves knowing God in a personal way and experiencing Christian fellowship. All of these things are vitally true, but in Ephesians 4:20-21 Paul's stress in his teaching about salvation was on the needed change in people's character to be like Christ (see Rom. 8:29; 2 Cor. 3:18).

Renewed individuals walk among God's people with an inward renunciation of their former way of life. In Galatians 2:20, Paul wrote: "I have been crucified with Christ; and it is no longer I who live, but Christ lives in me; and the life which I now live in the flesh I live by faith in the Son of God, who loved me, and delivered Himself up for me." Paul's affirmation is true for all believers. In Romans 6, Paul described the death to sin that takes place in believers' conversion and their living to righteousness that accompanies their faith. This spiritual transformation brings about not only an inward renunciation but also an inward restoration toward righteousness and holiness. Now, because we have put on the new person, we want to do what is right. We have been given a new heart and a new mind, and our entire way of life is being sanctified.[5]

Becoming What We Are (4:22-24)

Paul often described who believers are, and he described what they should become. He declared that Christians are free from sin, yet he exhorted them to put on the new self and perpetually to be renewed by the Holy Spirit's sanctifying work in their lives. The unregenerate old person had been nullified, and the new person had been put on. When a person puts his or her faith in Christ, that person at once is identified with Christ's death that already has happened. We need to identify fully with Christ's death by dying to sin. Life in the Spirit means that the Christian participates in Christ's risen life.

In the margin, write one area of your Christian experience in which you need to be renewed. Then list actions you will take to experience renewal.

As George Ladd wrote, "This is an eschatological fact that every believer should know (Rom. 6:2, 6), and on whose basis he is to consider himself alive to God."[6] In the old way of life, the dominion of sin had power. Redemptive change had occurred, and Paul exhorted believers to put on the new person and to yield themselves to righteousness.

How do we "lay aside the old self" (4:22) and "put on the new self" (4:24)? We must obey the command to become what we are in Christ. This is accomplished through yielding to the Spirit. The practical paradox is that freedom from sin comes through slavery to Christ. Even Paul's most affirmative statements about freedom are linked with lordship (see Gal. 5:1-24). Thus, Paul maintained that only two alternatives exist: (1) to have sin for our master or (2) to have God as Master. For

God to be our Master means a life of freedom from sin. Thus, true freedom comes only through authentic obedience. Jesus' life is a tangible portrayal and example of the new divine standard that Paul described in Ephesians 4:20-24 (see also Rom. 15:5; Col. 2:6-7).

Outward Application (4:25-32)

Ephesians 4:25-32 takes us into some practical applications of the Christian life. Paul gave five examples of what living the new life means. Holiness is not a mystical condition experienced in relation to God in isolation from people. A person cannot be holy and experience the new life in a vacuum; he or she can do so only in the context of relationship with others.

Truthfulness (4:25)

The five examples all include a negative command, a positive command, and a spiritual principle on which the commands are based. The first exhortation for people living the new life involves "laying aside falsehood." The positive command is to "speak truth." The spiritual principle for these commands rests in the unity of the body of Christ. "We are members of one another," creating an atmosphere of integrity that develops mutual trust within the church.

Dealing with Anger (4:26-27)

The second command focuses on the negative side: Do not lose your temper. The positive side is: Have righteous anger; that is, deal with anger rightly. The spiritual principle is to avoid giving the devil an opportunity to use our anger. For believers to be able to practice self-control and to deal with anger before it gets out of control is important. When we get angry in a way that hampers relationships with others, we are to deal with it in a timely fashion. That is what "do not let the sun go down on your anger" means.

Faith in Christ frees us to obey Him consistently. We are free to become what He has designed us to be, which includes having freedom from guilt and fear. Obedience to His will results in life that is meaningful and joyous.

Do you think honesty is a rare quality in our society? Why or why not?

85

"Be angry, and yet do not sin. . . . Let all bitterness and wrath and anger . . . be put away from you" (Eph. 4:26,31). How would you apply these verses to the situation portrayed above?

When is anger right and redemptive? When is it wrong and destructive? How will you use anger positively?

Because the devil is deceitful, we often have difficulty distinguishing righteous anger from losing our temper. When we fail to practice righteous anger, we disobey God and encourage the spread of evil. Jesus modeled righteous anger for us in John 2:13-17 when He cleansed the temple. Believers who seek to be prophetic in the fallen world will speak and act in righteous anger toward the degradation around us.

Responsible Labor (4:28)

The third exhortation is, "He who has been stealing must steal no longer." The negative command is: Stop stealing! The positive command is for believers to work with their own hands. The underlying principle is to have something to share with others. Believers are not to steal. This echoes the Eighth Commandment (Ex. 20:15). Of course, this has larger implications than refraining from taking things that do not belong to us. Stealing involves evading our responsibilities and not being faithful to our employers. Paul's antidote to this problem is to work hard with our hands. He taught that thieves can be changed to benefactors and contributors to society rather than sponging off others. The reason for working hard is that God wants us to share with people in need. Paul's admonition also indicates that we are responsible for taking care of our families' needs.

Honest work is honorable and scriptural. No one else should have a stronger work ethic than Christians. We should set the pace in quality of work, attitude in the workplace, and use of our earnings.

Careful Speech (4:29-30)

Paul's fourth command indicates that believers should not use their mouths in an evil manner. Rather, we are to use our words for good and positive purposes. The negative command is to refrain from unwholesome talk (v. 29). The positive command is to speak what is helpful in building up others (v. 29). The underlying principle is to benefit others. Jesus said that we will answer for every word we have spoken (see Matt. 12:36-37).

Using our mouths for good covers the two previous commands. Often in order to practice righteous anger, we will have to speak prophetic words. In this case, a true peacemaker may have to assume the role of peace breaker as a sacred obligation. We must speak wisely and not lose our temper or allow anger to grow and to develop into bitterness. We must do so because God has given His Spirit to us as a seal or a deposit. Thus, we are to be holy; the Holy Spirit is grieved by unholiness. The church is one; disunity grieves the Spirit. Christ's Spirit leads us to truth and is grieved by falsehood and

In what ways can we use words to benefit others? In the margin, list two ways you will do so during the next week.

Christians are to refrain from using unwholesome words and instead are to use words that will build others up.

heresy. We are to bring pleasure to the Holy Spirit, not to grieve Him.

Kindness (4:31-32)

The fifth command is that believers "be kind and compassionate to one another, forgiving each other" (v. 32). The positive exhortation is to be kind, compassionate, and forgiving; the negative command is to remove "bitterness, rage and anger, brawling and slander," and all malice (v. 31). The underlying principle is to reflect God's attitude toward us. Believers are not to be unkind but rather to be kind and loving. In all of our actions, we

Why is Christians' forgiving one another essential? What person do you need to forgive?

are to reflect the character of God who has forgiven us in Christ. In verse 32 Paul used a play on words when he admonished his readers to be kind (*chrestoi*) because of Christ (*christo*).

Paul offered six negative admonitions and three positive admonitions for living. We are to live and to speak in a way that builds up the body of Christ and helps to produce unity. We are not to grieve the Spirit; to do so causes a loss of joy, peace, and love in the new life. When we do any of the things listed in the negative expressions, they produce disharmony; a lack of trust, kindness, and righteousness results. When we put the positive commands into practice, they will help produce unity in the church (4:1-6). At the base of all Paul's commands is a God-centered spiritual foundation. Paul's ethic is God-centered. Ours must be the same. His ethic is based on sound doctrine. So must ours be. Let us recognize that good practice only arises out of sound doctrine, which we must grasp clearly and apply to all spheres of life and ministry.

Righteous Motivation (5:1-10)

Ephesians 5:1-10 focuses on the practice of Christian living as the outworking of the spiritual life. Paul greatly emphasized this theme in his writings, and we need this emphasis in our churches. We are to be imitators of God (5:1-5), to be pleasing to Him (5:6-10), and to live carefully (5:11-21).

Imitators of God (5:1-2)

In 5:1-5, Paul challenged his readers to be imitators of God. He had urged them to learn Christ (4:20-21) and not to grieve the Spirit (4:30). Paul's readers were to be imitators of God's love (vv. 1-2) and to walk in godliness (vv. 3-5). We cannot imitate God in power, knowledge, or presence. However, we can avoid self-indulgence and can practice self-sacrifice.

One way of imitating God is to have a forgiving spirit (4:32). We are to act as He has acted toward us. Then

The call to imitate God is one of the loftiest challenges in the Scriptures. In order to imitate Him, we must learn more about Him and from Him through Bible study and personal experience.

89

we are to exercise forgiving kindness and sacrificial love. Unbelievers give themselves up to sensuality (4:19); believers are to give themselves up to God. Sacrificial love becomes a sacrifice acceptable to God.[7]

Walk in Godliness (5:3-7)

As God's holy people, believers are to walk in godliness in all matters, especially in sexual matters. In our day, we need to affirm that the Christian view of sexuality is not negative. Sexuality is positive, not shameful. Sex is a good gift, high and holy when it is shared in the bonds of marriage as the Scriptures prescribe. As a well-known youth program has emphasized, true love indeed waits until marriage. This is God's plan and pattern.

All of God's gifts, including sex, are to be subjects of thanksgiving, not of "coarse joking" (v. 4, NIV). Such coarse joking degrades that which is good. Thanksgiving preserves the worth of God's gifts as blessings of a loving Creator. Believers are not to involve themselves in the harmful fellowship of ungodly people whose ruin is certain.

How can Christians maintain and promote biblical moral standards in a permissive society? In the margin, write one way you will do so.

God's wrath comes on "those who are disobedient" (literally, "sons of disobedience," v. 6). Viewed actively, God's wrath is His firm, ongoing opposition to evil; He is solidly and eternally opposed to everything that is contrary to His design and His nature. Viewed passively, God's wrath is the other side of His love: He allows people to choose, even to choose to reject Him and His way. He goes along with their choices, and the choices work their way out to disastrous, eternal consequences (see Rom. 1:24,26,28).

God's new community reflects the character of God's kingdom and the character of God's wrath. Paul contrasted two lifestyles: the godly and the greedy. Godliness involves self-denial, purity, and service. Greed is concerned with self, pride, and power. God wants His children to imitate Him and, thus, to please Him in all things.

Pleasing God (5:8-10)

Paul presented the Christian's highest duty: to please God. Today, most people are confused and seek happiness as an end in itself. Instead, we need to recognize that happiness is a by-product of obedience. As righteous persons, we must stand for righteousness. Because we have believed the truth, we must do the truth. Producing and practicing "the fruit of the light" (v. 9) means that we are to do good because in Christ we have been made good.

The basic principle involved in 5:8-10 is that believers must recognize and do God's will. When Paul exhorted his readers to "find out what pleases the Lord" (v. 10, NIV), he had in mind believers' giving their lives for others and not pleasing themselves. This motive makes duty and Christian living a delight. It invests service with joy. God can strengthen our wills and can set our hearts at ease when our goal in life is to do His will and not to please ourselves.

What part does a deep desire to please God play in your daily life? What do you think pleases Him?

Spiritual Illumination (5:11-21)

Christians are to be careful (the central exhortation of the section, 5:15). Believers are to have consistent conduct. They are to grow in moral denunciation (vv. 11-14), temporal redemption (vv. 15-16), and spiritual illumination (vv. 17-21).

Careful Christianity (5:11-17)

As imitators of God who seek to make the most of their time and to live a life that is pleasing to Him, believers must ask how to overcome the world's approach to living. Careful Christians do more than abstain from evil. They denounce the deeds of darkness as unfruitful, shameful, and not worthwhile.

How can believers, in the spirit of Christ, expose and oppose the evil around us?

Three principles can help guide us as we seek to become careful Christians. First, we should not allow our context to weaken us, for it is shaped by the ways of the world. Second, we must not be deceived by the persuasiveness of people around us. Sometimes when we are enticed to evil, God seems distant and unreal to us. We need to be able to manifest careful self-control. Satan will attempt to cause us to forget God; so we constantly must put on the mind of Christ (see Phil 2:5). Third, we constantly must be taking heed about how we are conducting ourselves. We must not be confused or deceived.

We will not be deceived when we stand firm, enabled by and filled with God's Spirit. Also, because we have been able to stand on one occasion does not mean that we are guaranteed victory again and again; for Satan and his demonic hosts will come again. We face sights and sounds daily that dull our spiritual sensitivity. Paul called for believers to be careful in their response.

If we characteristically fall into a life of immorality or greed, we are indicating that the objects of our affection are things other than God. In that sense, we are not too different from idolaters. Instead of worshiping God, we worship things around us. Paul's words in Ephesians 5:15-16 are a solemn warning that we should be wise and careful in all things. We must ask about our goals and motivations to see whether we are seeking to please God in all things.

Careful Christians also redeem the time. "Making the most of your time" involves aggressively seizing and buying up the time. Time is not neutral; it can be evil if it is not invested for good (see Ps. 90). We do not have equal resources or abilities, but we all have the same amount of time to invest for matters of eternal worth.

In 5:1-17, Paul described two philosophies of life: the world's and God's. The world's lifestyle is characterized by moral and spiritual darkness. The philosophy for

Christians must look for and even create opportunities to be redemptive in our society. Opportunities for witness and ministry present themselves daily. We must act on them.

godly living is characterized by moral and spiritual light, and its goal is to imitate God and His love. The motivation for living by the world's philosophy is to please self. The motivation for godly living is to please God. Living according to the world results in carelessness and recklessness. A life that pleases God is a life that suppresses selfishness, denounces immorality, and redeems the time with the Spirit's help.

Often I tell my children to be careful. The kind of care that Paul wrote about is more than being cautious. It includes a conscience sensitive to spiritual truths. It also involves a diligent effort to put these truths into practice.

Filled with the Spirit (5:18-21)

Christians are not to get drunk on wine, which leads to dissipation. Instead, we are to be filled with the Holy Spirit. Paul's imperative in verse 18 is a command for us to obey. Paul contrasted the differences between being under the influence of wine that leads to dissipation and life in the Spirit that results in joyful living. Wine is a depressant; the Spirit is a stimulant. Wine leads to debauchery, making us less than human. The Spirit makes us more like Christ, thus making us fully human. Wine brings an artificial merriment; the Spirit leads us to sober gladness and worship with sacred song. Wine can cause illness, but the Spirit produces a sense of well-being.

Paul's exhortation is an imperative, but the verb forms of the words translated "do not get drunk" and "be filled" are plural. Thus, the commands refer not merely to the individual but to the corporate community of faith. The Spirit's fullness is demonstrated in spiritual understanding, praise, and thanksgiving that are constant and comprehensive. The church that is filled with the Spirit will be characterized by praise and thanksgiving to God.

The highest praise we can offer God is a life that consistently reflects His character. Do you agree or disagree? Why?

Beyond that will be the evidence of self-control, up-building fellowship, and mutual submission.

In contrast to wine, which the cult of Dionysus regarded as a means to inspiration, the Spirit leads us to know God's will and to live a life of self-control.[8] Paul also wrote that when we praise God and sing hymns, we do it one to another as well as to God so as to build up one another in the faith. Another evidence of being Spirit-filled is the practice of mutual submission, living in deference to one another (see Rom. 12:10). Mutual submission is the opposite of rudeness, haughtiness, and self-assertion. This lifestyle can be achieved only with the Spirit's enabling power "out of reverence for Christ" (v. 21, NIV).

Do you consider courtesy to be a quality of Christian living? Why or why not?

[1]See David S. Dockery, "New Nature and Old Nature," *Dictionary of Paul and His Letters* (Downers Grove, Ill.: InterVarsity, 1993), 628-29.

[2]R. Kent Hughes, *Ephesians: The Mystery of the Body of Christ* (Wheaton: Crossway, 1990), 140-42.

[3]Markus Barth, "Ephesians," vol. 34A in *The Anchor Bible* (New York: Doubleday & Company, 1974), 504, 530.

[4]John R. W. Stott, *God's New Society: The Message of Ephesians* (Downers Grove, Ill.: InterVarsity, 1979), 178-83.

[5]See David S. Dockery, "An Outline of Paul's View of the Spiritual Life: Foundation for an Evangelical Spirituality," *Criswell Theological Review* 3 (1989): 327-39.

[6]George E. Ladd, *A Theology of the New Testament* (Grand Rapids: Wm. B. Eerdmans Publishing Co., 1974), 486.

[7]See Curtis Vaughan, *Ephesians: A Study Guide Commentary* (Grand Rapids: Zondervan Publishing House, 1977), 105.

[8]See the discussion in Stott, *God's New Society*, 204.

Chapter 8

Christian Relationships

Ephesians 5:22—6:9

A. Wives and Husbands (5:22-33)
B. Children and Parents (6:1-4)
C. Masters and Servants (6:5-9)

Many people today think that the last couple who
lived happily ever after was in a movie or a story book.
Actually, entering marriage is one of the most difficult
and complex transitions of life. The new couple,
friends, and family want to see the event as a happy,
joyful time. The new bride and groom may see their
marriage as a solution to the problem of loneliness or of
family hassles. The parents may respond: "Finally, he
settled down"; or, "Now, she has someone else to take
care of her."

Marriages create challenges for which many people
are not prepared. Statistics indicate that these challenges often are overwhelming. The Scriptures can
guide people to move beyond wishfulness, fantasies, and
unrealistic expectations to fulfill their mutual responsibilities in marriage. Let Paul's inspired words guide us.

Wives and Husbands (5:22-33)

Ephesians 5:22-33 introduces a new kind of relationship
characterized by the basic principle of submissiveness.
Social relationships are similar to those that govern the
church's life in community. In 5:19-21, Paul listed re-

Today, mar-
riages are sub-
ject to increas-
ing pressures.
Finances, dual
careers, and
problems with
children are
only a few of
the pressures.
An added ten-
sion is the view
that marriage is
a temporary
arrangement.
Believers are to
set the pace in
working at
growing good
marriages.

sults of being filled with the Spirit: (1) speaking to one another with psalms, hymns, and spiritual songs (v. 19); (2) singing and making music in the heart to the Lord (v. 19); (3) giving thanks for everything (v. 20); and (4) mutually submitting to one another out of reverence for Christ (v. 21). Paul then applied the principle of mutual submissiveness to relationships between wives and husbands (5:22-33), children and parents (6:1-4), and servants and masters (6:5-9).

ILLUSTRATION BY JAMES FINCH

Ephesians 5:33 teaches that a Christian husband should "love his wife as he loves himself, and the wife must respect her husband."

A General Principle

Verse 21 serves as a hinge to connect what is prior with what follows. Grammatically, the participial phrase in verse 21 (literally, "submitting yourselves") goes with 5:18-20. However, the content of 5:22-33 depends on the principle of submission in 5:21.[1] Each family member should yield his or her rights for the other's good. This means no one is to coerce the other; each family member voluntarily accepts this discipline. Family members should not think of themselves more highly than they ought (compare Phil. 2:1-4). Delusions of superiority are dissipated. The gospel places all relationships on a revolutionary new footing because all believers are submissive to the Lord.[2]

What do you think Christians' submitting to one another means? In what ways can we do this?

The Responsibility of Christian Wives (5:22-24,33)

While Paul began the instructions to households by a plea for mutual submissiveness, the exhortations to submissiveness are not mutual. Similar to Colossians 3:18—4:1, this Ephesians passage specifically directs wives to be submissive to their (*idios:* "one's own") husbands. The distinctive feature here is that the relationship between husband and wife is compared with that between Christ and the church.

No verb is in the original language of verse 22. The imperative "be subject" is understood from verse 21. Paul addressed wives first. They were to be submissive to their husbands. Paul stressed the exclusiveness of the marriage relationship. The verb translated "be subject" (adopted from v. 21) is in a grammatical form that means voluntary submission. No external coercion is involved.

What do you think wives' being submissive to their husbands means? Do husbands automatically have a right to this submissiveness? Why?

The submission is governed by the phrase "as to the Lord" (v. 22). Christian wives' submission to their husbands is one aspect of their obedience to Christ.

97

If we can get beyond certain red-flag or trigger words in Ephesians 5:22-23, we can see God's beautiful model for wives in contemporary Christian marriages. These words are *submission* and *head*. Their meaning becomes clear in light of the entire context and of the command for husbands to love their wives (5:25).[3]

First, as we seek to understand the meaning of submission we need to look at what submission *is not*. Today, Paul often is seen as an oppressor who championed a subservient role for women. People advocating this view reject any idea of submission because they think it magnifies chauvinism and reduces the status of women; but Paul's meaning, understood in its context, points us in a different direction.

Within the Christian community are some people who stress the subordinate role of women in the Christian home. These people want to establish a chain of command in which husbands have absolute authority over their wives. Often, under the guise of submission, women within such a system seek to manipulate their husbands. Other wives give the appearance of submitting but really do not give themselves totally to their husbands. Both of these views fail to produce the partnership God wants in Christian marriages.

Submission *is* a person's yielding his or her own rights and losing self for another. Submission is patterned after Christ (Phil. 2:5-8) and reflects the essence of the gospel. Underlying the general principal of submission are four important themes: (1) the dignity and the worth of all members of the church; (2) the equality of all members of the new community; (3) the unity of all believers; and (4) the need for mutual submission among believers.

Our world is receptive to terms like *self-assertion* and *self-actualization*. We cower from terms like *submission* and *self-denial* because we tend to be self-seeking and self-serving. Yet Paul's words, like those of Jesus in

Marriage is described as a partnership. In what ways is this true?

98

Mark 8:34-35, affirm that self-fulfillment comes through giving ourselves for one another, considering others' needs above our own self-interests. Paul called for a wife's submission in a setting where all persons are valued and where the needs and the interests of a wife's husband are more important than getting her way.

Submission is an ethical emphasis throughout the New Testament. It characterizes the sacrificial life of service to which Christ calls the entire church. Paul particularly appealed to wives to follow the Lord in their relationship to their husbands. Again, the verbal form indicates an earnest inner appeal that the husband cannot externally force. Paul restated his appeal in Ephesians 5:33, calling for wives to respect their husbands. This message is relevant and significant for both ancient and contemporary marriages.

Wives are to submit to their husbands, not because to do so fulfills the status quo but because submission distinguishes the lifestyle of all Christians. When wives live this way, submission is not coerced by divine sanction or inherent permanence. Rather, submission is based on mutual respect, affirmation, and service. Christian marriages have no high or low positions. In the new society that Christ's reconciling work created, a new order has been born in which all participants regard themselves as servants of one Lord—Christ— and yield themselves to one another because of Him.

In the margin, list three ways a husband and wife can express mutual respect and affirmation. What happens when these expressions become a consistent part of the relationship?

Verse 23 presents the marriage relationship as a reflection of Christ and the church. The church as Christ's bride acknowledges His authority and seeks to please Him in every respect. When marriage is viewed in light of Christ and His church, wives are able to understand their submission to their husbands as an aspect of their common obligation to the Lord.

Though other cultures in New Testament times required wives to submit to their husbands, Paul explained the Christian relationship in terms of a common union in the Lord. Wives are to live out their commitment to Christ in their relationships with their husbands. The exhortation to be submissive means to be humble and unselfish. It means a person's yielding his or her own rights and considering others' needs first. Submission is not the same thing as obedience. The word "obey" is in 6:1 (children are to "obey" parents) and 6:5 (servants are to "be obedient" to masters) but not in 5:22-24. How does this principle relate to the responsibilities of Christian husbands?

The Responsibilities of Christian Husbands (5:25-33)

Paul turned to the duties of husbands. The society in which Paul wrote recognized the duties of wives to husbands but not necessarily of husbands to wives. As in Colossians 3:19, Paul exhorted husbands to love their wives; but Ephesians presents Christ's self-sacrificing love for the church as the pattern for the husband's love for his wife. What a radical difference between Paul's command and his culture! The ancient world was primarily a man's world; so this difference was most apparent in the home.

Among the Jews, wives sometimes were little more than their husband's property. The Greeks generally restricted the women to their own quarters and often separated the men from the women at mealtimes. Paul's instructions were in striking contrast to these practices. Husbands were to love their wives continually as Christ loves the church. The tense of the Greek word translated "love" indicates a love that continues. Love is more than family affection or sexual passion. Rather it is a deliberate attitude, leading to action, that concerns itself with another's

Why is love in the Christian sense of determined good-will an essential part of marriage? Is it as important as romantic love? Why?

well-being. A husband should love his wife: (1) as Christ loved the church (vv. 25-27); (2) as his own body (vv. 28-30); and (3) with a love transcending all other human relationships (vv. 31-33).[4]

A husband's love for his wife is sacrificial like Christ's. Christ's love for the church is a self-sacrificing love, and Paul implied that the same love is to be true of a husband's love for his wife. The context, not necessarily the word itself (*agapate*), informs us of the sacrificial nature of the husband's love.

Verses 26-27 explain more fully the result of Christ's atonement for the church: to make the church holy and pure. The purpose of Christ's giving Himself up for the church is the church's sanctification and cleansing with water. While some people try to find ancient rituals of the fertility cults or some Gnostic schemes as the background for Paul's words, the Old Testament portrayal of Israel as the bride of Yahweh provides all of the background necessary.[5]

When husbands love their wives as Christ loved the church, the husbands give up their personal rights for the good of their wives. This sacrificial love provides security and freedom for a marriage. It is a solemn picture of covenant love.

Christ loves the church and one day will present it beautiful, glorious, holy, and without blemish. To this constructive end Christ has been working and is working. The bride, "the church" (v. 27), does not make herself presentable; the Bridegroom beautifies her in order to present her to Himself. Christ's love for the church cleanses and sanctifies it; His love is designed for the church's liberation and perfection.

The implications of Christ's loving headship are clear. Christ does not crush the church. He sacrificed Himself to serve it. In the same way, a husband never should exercise his headship to stifle his wife or to frustrate her from being herself. Rather, his love for her will lead him in another direction. He will give himself up for her so that she may develop her full potential under

When a husband has an attitude of self-giving love like that of Christ, his wife can respect him and follow his leadership.

101

God and thus become more fully herself, the kind of person and wife God wants her to be. Headship does not imply kingship but companionship.

In verse 28, Paul turned to his second comparison. Husbands ought to love their wives as being one flesh with themselves. The original language points to their moral obligation. So intimate is the relationship between husband and wife that they become "one flesh" (v. 31).

For a husband to love his wife is to love himself. He is not to treat her as a piece of property. He is to regard her as part of himself. "No one ever hated his own flesh" (v. 29). The phrase expresses something characteristically true. The comparison is applied further in verses 29b-30. The context indicates that Paul's thought remained focused on the intimacy of the church's relationship with Christ. In God's purpose, a wife becomes part of her husband's life; and the husband nourishes and cherishes his wife. Similarly, as a wife becomes a part of her husband so members of the church become a part of the Lord. They become part of His own life; He has joined them to Himself. Paul stressed the closeness of this relationship, and his emphasis is similar to Jesus' words about the relationship of branches to a vine (compare John 15).

On first sight, Paul seems to have descended from the lofty standard of Christ's love to the low standard of self-love; but he reminded Christian couples of their oneness, their "one-flesh" relationship. For this reason, a husband's obligation to cherish his wife as he does his own body is more than a helpful guide for daily living. He does so as a symbol and an expression of the sacred marital union. When a husband and his wife have this spiritual, emotional, and physical oneness with each other, they evidence true love.

The final comparison in verses 31-33 portrays a love that transcends all other human relationships. Paul re-

How can husbands and wives help each other realize their potential?

ferred to Genesis 2:24, which is God's initial statement in the Scriptures regarding marriage. The Old Testament appeal substantiated Paul's argument. The marriage commitment takes precedence over every other human relationship and for this reason is regarded as secure from violation. The phrase "the two shall become one flesh" (v. 31; Gen. 2:24) means "closely joined." It hallows the biblical standard of marital relations and excludes polygamy and adultery. What is primarily a divine ordinance graciously and lovingly is designed for mutual satisfaction and delight.

Verse 32 appeals to the fuller meaning of Genesis 2:24. Startlingly, the mystery wrapped up in Genesis 2:24 was realized when Christ came to win His bride, the church, by giving Himself for her on the cross. The likeness of the marital union to this higher spiritual relationship gives marriage its deepest significance. This mystery refers to the relationship between Christ and the church, a mystery to which Paul had been given divine insight (see Eph. 3:3-9). Ephesians 5:22-33 calls on husbands to measure up to the ideal of Christ in His love for the church and calls on wives to measure up to the church in its devotion to Christ.

Verse 33 concludes the discussion of marriage with a practical summary. The *Good News Bible*[6] emphasizes the practical nature of Paul's conclusion, translating: "But it [Gen. 2:24, GNB] also applies to you." The husband's responsibility is to "love his own wife." The wife's responsibility is to "respect her husband." Such respect is self-initiated, not forced. Paul's command also assumes that the husband will love his wife in such a way as to be worthy of such respect.

Paul proclaimed that the permanent, intimate love in marriage transcends all other human relationships. Unfortunately, we often mistake infatuation for true love and offer inadequate substitutes for love. We must realize that love grows and that growth takes time.

Husbands and wives are extensions of each other. This does not mean that one person's personality is swallowed up by the other. It means that each marriage partner is a vital part of the other; neither is whole without the other. Both find their completion in each other.

Why do you think Paul instructed husbands to "love" their wives and urged wives to "respect" their husbands?

103

Infatuation may be attracted to one characteristic in a person; love grows out of the total personality. Infatuation is self-centered. Love is other-centered and concerned with the other person's total well-being. Love offers true identification with the other person.

Husbands sometimes offer substitutes in the place of authentic, sacrificial love. In our day, we are accustomed to such substitutes. We have artificial flavoring, substitute foods, veneer instead of solid wood, vinyl in the place of leather, and so on. However, substitutes in the marriage relationship are inadequate and unacceptable.

A husband's love that transcends all other human relationships will not be satisfied with merely providing his wife's physical and material needs. Instead he will share his life with her. He will not substitute intimidation for leadership. He will not smother her but will honor and appreciate her. Thus, the husband's ultimate responsibility is to love his wife with a Christlike love.

Children and Parents 6:1-4

I remember clearly when our first son was born on September 9, 1979. The time was a Sunday morning in Dallas, Texas. After dinner on Saturday night, my wife began to experience the early stages of labor. That Sunday morning brought one of the truly outstanding events of our lives, for God gave us a wonderful little boy named Jonathan. While years have passed since that Sunday morning, in many ways it seems like yesterday. Since that time, God has blessed our lives with two other sons, Benjamin and Timothy.

When I reflect on the challenges and the stresses that we have faced since the boys' births, I sometimes wonder how we have survived these years. On other days, as I recall the events of these past years, it seems only a moment ago that God first blessed our lives with children. People have told me to savor every moment and

104

not to rush through the child-rearing years. That is good advice. Children grow up; and in no time, they are on their own. The realization that we have such a short time to rear our children motivates us to make the most of the time (see Eph. 5:16) and to follow God's advice about rearing children.

We need to read, hear, and heed Paul's wise words in Ephesians 6:1-4. Interestingly, Paul followed the guidelines of the ethical teaching of his day in focusing on children first. His offering a reciprocal word to parents is surprising. We must not and cannot ignore this reciprocal word. Both children and parents need to hear Paul's instructions. I believe that Paul's addressing children indicates that he anticipated children would be present in the church meeting when the letter initially was read.

Responsibility of Children (6:1-3)

Paul's initial concerns were for children to be responsible to their parents. He called for children to be obedient as taught in natural law, in the Mosaic law, and in the gospel. He instructed children to obey (a different word from the term for submission that was used in the husband/wife relationship [5:21-24]). Obedience involves recognition of authority. Children are to obey because to do so is right and because they are in the Lord.

No clash of loyalties is involved in Paul's command. Paul assumed the context of believing families and appealed to the Ten Commandments. Exodus 20:12 and Deuteronomy 5:16 exhort children to obey their parents. Paul did not offer this exhortation as a threat but gave the command as one that contains a promise. The promise is general, not one that can be individualized; and it points to the kind of stability that is created in societies where children are taught to obey their

Rearing children has become increasingly difficult. Ever-mounting peer pressure competes with the home for allegiance to values. Christian parents must stress Christian values and must model them.

What are wider repercussions of children's failing to learn obedience in the home? List some of these in the margin.

105

parents. A healthy respect for authority provided the framework and the foundation for Paul to offer this twofold word to children: obey and honor.

Responsibility of Parents (6:4)

Perhaps more important than children's obedience is the role that parents have in the family. Parents are to provide the classroom—the environment, the setting—in which children learn to obey. Parents have responsibility both to discipline and to instruct their children. Paul indicated that fathers are to take the lead in this responsibility, though the word translated "fathers" in

Both children and parents need to read, hear, and heed the wise, inspired instructions in Ephesians 6:1-4.

verse 4 also can mean "parents." One of the goals of child-rearing is for parents to help children come to the place of accepting God's rule in their lives through discipline and instruction in a real and a personal way. In order to bring this about, parents need to recognize that children are gifts from God (see Ps. 127:4-5).

Parents are to realize that children are gifts to return to God. Also, parents are to recognize that children need love, significance, and security. Parents are to give needed discipline and instruction with tenderness. They need to recognize their responsibility for dis-

> Can any other persons or institutions make up for the home's failure to instruct and to discipline children? Explain your answer.

ciplining their children, which is not an arbitrary kind of discipline or something done out of anger. Paul's words are a negative warning: Parents are not to abuse their children, and they are not to create a sense of bitterness that will lead to rebellion. In fact, parents must recognize their own need for ongoing training. The goal of discipline and instruction is to establish boundaries and guidelines for children.

Proverbs 22:6 provides a helpful word. The writer encouraged parents to raise up a child in his or her way. Wise parents know that children are different and that not all nonconformity is self-styled rebellion. The goal of Christian parenting is to train children according to their interests or desires. Proverbs 22:6 could be translated "according to his or her bent." The goal is to help children become obedient and godly in whatever God-honoring direction their lives may take.

Edna Ferber's novel *Giant* has an interesting story. She wrote about a Texas millionaire named Jordan Benedict. Benedict owned a 2.5-million-acre cattle ranch. His wife was miserable, and he was furious because his young son refused to ride horses. In the novel, Benedict said: "I rode [horses] before I could walk." His wife responded, "That was you. This is another person. Maybe he just doesn't like horses." The Texas millionaire responded: "He's a Benedict and I'm going to make a horseman out of him if I have to tie him to do it."[7]

For what reasons is trying to relive our lives through our children detrimental to them? List reasons in the margin.

Neither Paul's words nor any other words in the Scriptures encourage us to force our children into a preconceived mold. Our responsibility, at formal times and at informal times, is to instruct them in God's ways so that their lives can be holy and pleasing in God's sight.

The instructions in Deuteronomy 6:6-7 remain helpful for putting Paul's words into practice. Parents are to have formal times of instruction, designated times for reading, and scheduled times for doing things together. Parents also are to take advantage of informal times, such as mealtimes and special situations when the children ask: "What should we do?" During these informal times children often learn more than in formal times, for often more is caught than is taught. Parents need to watch what they say around their children and to speak encouraging, upbuilding, and healing words.

Masters and Servants (6:5-9)

Paul still was concerned with the Christian household, for many servants were employed in the home. About one-third of the population of Rome were slaves. That they were addressed in the context of the church community indicates plenty. They were treated alongside their masters as equal members of the believing community. Remember that Tychicus, who brought the Ephesian Letter to the churches in Asia Minor, also carried the letter about Onesimus (a slave) to Philemon. Paul's words did not lead to immediate freedom for slaves. However, when biblical principles of human freedom and human worth were put into practice, slavery was abolished.

The New Testament did not condemn slavery, but it did not condone slavery either. New Testament Christians were politically powerless. Slavery systems, as bad and as dehumanizing as they were, nevertheless were quite different from slavery as practiced in the United States in the 19th century. By the early part of the first century A.D., slaves had rights to marry, to travel, to own property, and to be tried in a court of law.

Paul wrote that slaves and masters were equal before God. The Roman law might discriminate but heavenly justice does not. Paul's words to servants and masters in this context provided the groundwork for a new brotherhood in the new society.

Paul's words can be translated into today's context to apply more specifically to employees and to employers

Christian parents are responsible for providing children with a sound basis for making decisions and for giving them increasing freedom to decide. Loving, caring guidance all along the way will help children mature in their choices.

● ● ● ● ● ● ● ● ● ● ● ● ●

in the work relationship, though this context is not an extension of the household. That Paul mentioned slaves is startling when we recognize that Plato did not mention them in *The Republic*, although about 60,000,000 people were slaves at that time. Paul appealed to slaves to do their work as to the Lord and to recognize that ultimately they were servants of the Lord. Today, Christian workers often need to seek to serve the Lord in their work. In the congregation, employees and employers stand on equal ground before the Lord. Employers can expect employees to give good work; employees can expect employers to give fair wages in exchange for good work.

In what ways can any job, no matter how seemingly menial, be offered to Christ as service to Him? Should a job be more than making a living? Explain your answer.

What responsibilities do employers have toward employees? How should a Christian employer seek to demonstrate his relationship to Christ?

Employers must be in business not merely to produce profit but also with a concern for their employees' well-being. Both Christian employees and employers need a wholeheartedness to the task that seeks to translate their service as faithful work in line with God's will. A person can recognize that Jesus is Lord of all, whether he or she is the gas station attendant or the president of the oil company. Employees and employers need to share a mutual respect. Employers need to learn to relate to employees in a non-threatening way—not as an exercise of the powerful over the powerless but in the context of Christian relationships.

---

[1]The *New American Standard Bible* treats verse 21 as a dependent clause, the conclusion of the sentence that began at verse 18. The paragraph is divided between verse 21 and verse 22. The *New International Version* treats verse 21 as a complete sentence and a separate paragraph with the subject heading between verse 20 and verse 21. The *New International Version Study Bible*, however, treats verse 21 as a complete sentence and a separate paragraph; but the subject heading is placed between verse 21 and verse 22.

[2]A. Skevington Wood, "Ephesians," in *The Expositor's Bible Commentary*, vol. 11 (Grand Rapids: Zondervan Publishing House, 1978), 75.

[3]Diana R. and David E. Garland, *Marriage: For Better or For Worse?* (Nashville: Broadman Press, 1989), 90-91.

[4]Curtis Vaughn, *Ephesians: A Study Guide Commentary* (Grand Rapids: Zondervan Publishing House, 1977), 117-18.

[5]Andrew T. Lincoln, "Ephesians," vol. 42 in *Word Biblical Commentary* (Dallas: Word, 1990), 357-63.

[6]This quotation is from the *Good News Bible, the Bible in Today's English Version.* Old Testament: Copyright © American Bible Society 1976; New Testament: Copyright © American Bible Society 1966, 1971, 1976. Used by permission.

[7]Edna Ferber, *Giant* (New York: Pocket Books, 1954), 290.

Chapter 9

Spiritual Conflict

Ephesians 6:10-24

> A. Principalities and Powers 6:10-17
> B. Communal Nature of Prayer 6:18-20
> C. Concluding Remarks 6:21-24

The power of the evil against which believers struggle is evident everywhere in our world. Greed, violence, lust for power, and wanton destruction are rampant. The struggle is real and is deadly serious. Only the spiritual resources God provides can help us win the cosmic war.

"Our struggle is not against flesh and blood" (Eph. 6:12). This struggle is often too great for people in today's materialistic, secularistic world to handle. The enemy with whom we struggle in spiritual conflict is powerful and deceitful. The devil particularly singles out believers because they are followers of Christ. Satan hates Christ and the church. As Martin Luther penned in his famous hymn, "A Mighty Fortress is Our God":

For still our ancient foe
    Doth seek to work us woe;
His craft and power are great,
    And, armed with cruel hate,
On earth is not His equal.

The Prince of Darkness grim,
    We tremble not for him;
His rage we can endure,
    For lo, his doom is sure;
One little word shall fell him.[1]

Paul brought his readers to a jolting reality as he concluded his majestic letter. We have seen the graciousness of salvation and the giftedness of God's people for service. The letter instructs us about happy living in

112

the home before it awakens us to the spiritual reality of the conflict that exists in the Christian life. Paul painted a chilling picture of the cosmic war raging between Satan and God's people. We can ignore this reality, or we can overreact to it; either way, we will miss God's teaching.

We need to be awakened to the amoral and the immoral practices that characterize our world. Behind these practices are the enemy's satanic influences.

The cults, the occult, the New Age movement, the challenge to traditional morals, and the attack against the family are examples of the spiritual battle described in Ephesians 6:10-20. Paul described the spiritual battle that takes place against evil in the heavenly realm. Ephesians points us to this unseen world. Paul's words that call us to battle underscore the spiritual warfare's cosmic scope. The section 6:10-20 deals with defensive and offensive armor. During Paul's imprisonment, he no doubt saw many Roman soldiers. The Holy Spirit may have used this sight to inspire Paul's thinking to write this section.

> Why do you think cults are attracting people who have backgrounds in the Christian faith? How can we combat the influence of cults?

Principalities and Powers (6:10-17)

Some present-day Christians err by becoming preoccupied with the demonic and the spiritual conflict or by ignoring or disbelieving it. Believers of a former day gave significant attention to such warfare, as evidenced by William Gurnall's 1669 volume. The Puritan minister's deep reflections provide balanced guidance for the warfare we face. He wrote: "In heaven we shall appear, not in Armour, but in Robes of Glory; but here they are to be worn night and day, we must walk, work, and sleep in them, or else we are not true Souldiers of Christ."[2]

> Why is feeling that we do not need God's armor dangerous?

113

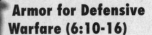
ILLUSTRATION BY JEFF PRESTON

Armor for Defensive Warfare (6:10-16)

Verse 10 calls for Christians to take a strong stand. In 6:10-14, three times Paul called for Christians to stand against the devil's schemes. He initially challenged his readers to be aware of and to stand strong against the devil's schemes (v. 11) and the evil day (v. 13), the time of special spiritual pressure. Believers need stability and character to withstand the crisis. The whole armor of God portrays Christian character.

The threefold call to stand is a recognition of our lack of stability.[3] Paul realized that Christians can be easy prey for Satan. However, the armor and the weapons are God's. God shares them with us. Our responsibility is to exercise them. Of course, our primary source of strength is Christ. Paul portrayed our enemies as being on every side: right, left, front, and back. So also must our armor be on every side.

In the margin, list situations in which Christians must stand firm in our day. What are ways we can express our strong stand?

114

The Belt (6:14)

The defensive armor that Paul described in these verses includes five parts. The first piece of armor is the belt ("girded" NASB), the enabling nature of truth. The belt signifies that Christians are to resist lying and false doctrine. The Greek construction for "truth" in verse 14 could point to the Truth—Jesus Christ (John 14:6)—or to moral, experiential truth in general. Both are applicable. We are to tighten our belts and to prepare ourselves for action and for challenges to the truth. At no place are we more out of line with society's priorities than to stand for absolute truth. That Jesus is "the way, and the truth, and the life" (John 14:6) must be the church's bedrock and convictional foundation, not merely a matter of religious preference as our society would like. Standing for truth in relationships, morality, and doctrine are the church's mandatory responsibilities.

The Breastplate (6:14)

The second piece of armor is the breastplate, which is the covering quality of righteousness. Paul's idea of righteousness emphasizes justification (see Rom. 3:21-26; 8:31-39), our right-standing before God, and the resulting moral righteousness and transformation that accompany this truth (see Rom. 6:1-23; Eph. 4:24; 5:9). We are to resist accusations of conscience, despondency, and inconsistency because no one can bring a charge against God's elect (Rom. 8:33-34). The breastplate covered both the front and the back, and we are to recognize that Christ's righteousness covers us completely before God.

Believers must know the truth, speak the truth, and insist on the truth. We know Christ—the Truth—through personal experience and Bible study. His grace and strength enable us to live the truth in a time when truth is rare.

115

The Boot (6:15)

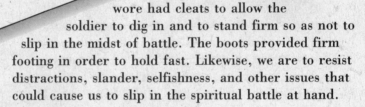

The third piece of armor that Paul identified was the boot (sandal), the stabilizing quality of peace. The boots that Roman soldiers wore had cleats to allow the soldier to dig in and to stand firm so as not to slip in the midst of battle. The boots provided firm footing in order to hold fast. Likewise, we are to resist distractions, slander, selfishness, and other issues that could cause us to slip in the spiritual battle at hand.

What are some prevalent temptations that cause Christians to slip today? How can we reject these temptations?

The Shield (6:16)

The fourth piece of armor is the shield, the protective ability of faith. The shield was three feet by two feet and was used to protect the soldier from the fiery darts that could penetrate and burn him. For the Roman soldiers, these fiery darts were as devastating as chemical warfare in our day. As the shield could protect, so our faith can resist prayerlessness and can protect us from doubts and discouragement. We are to recognize that faith pleases God and is a characteristic sign of God's people (see Heb. 11).

The Helmet (6:17)

Paul identified the fifth piece of defensive armor as the helmet, the encouraging nature of salvation. The helmet signified assurance of future and final victory. Thus our salvation is secure; and we have assurance in this life to resist fear, cowardice, and disappointment. This word picture reminds us that pointing to our final victory in Christ rescues us from the tyranny of the immediate.[4]

The five pieces of defensive armor prepare us for the challenges we will face. Challenges with which we must deal each day in addition to the kind of issues listed previously are the temptations to be anxious instead of praying (see Phil. 4:6-7). Instead of living the Christian life consistently, we are prone toward peaks and valleys. We are tempted to speak when we should be silent and to be silent when we should speak, confusing humility and pride. We are prone to please people and to fall into the trap of worldliness. We fail to distinguish anger from righteous anger and flippancy from proper fun. Church members often fail to distinguish the difference between being pupils of the church and being critics of the church and its theology. Paul called for believers to put on the whole armor, which points to its divine nature more than to its completeness. The armor's divine character prepares us for special pressure and undergirds stability in our character so that we can stand against evil and the principalities and powers.

> Is faith static—once you have it, it is constant; or is it dynamic—waning and growing? Explain your answer. In the margin, list ways you can strengthen your faith.

The Offensive Armor (6:17)

The offensive armor included only one weapon. The sword represented the gospel and God's written Word.[5] We are to recognize that the sword is spiritual in its origination. The sword that Paul described was a short sword used in close combat. This picture underscores the Scriptures' power and emphasizes our need to know God's Word. God's Word serves as a guide for godly living, provides strength for the weary, gives instruction and understanding in life, brings renewal to our soul and spirit, and leads to joy and delight. The psalmist described God's Word as

> In what ways is the Bible an offensive weapon in our spiritual warfare?

117

more precious than silver and gold; as wonderful, fully trustworthy, true, established, and eternal (see Ps. 119). The right response to God's Word is to love it and to meditate on it all day long (Ps. 119:97) because it is a lamp to our feet and a light to our path (Ps. 119:105).

Because of the Scriptures' design, content and origin, they can be described as "trustworthy" (2 Tim. 2:11), "confirmed" (Heb. 2:3), abiding "forever" (1 Pet. 1:24-25), and "sure" (2 Pet. 1:19). People who build their lives on God's Word will not be disappointed and will be prepared for the evil one's schemes. God gave His written Word to instruct and to encourage believers (Rom. 15:4), to lead people to saving faith (2 Tim. 3:15), to guide people toward godliness (2 Tim. 3:16), and to equip believers for good works and stability in the spiritual battle (see 2 Tim. 3:17; Eph. 6:17). Without this offensive weapon, we would be unprepared for Satan's wicked schemes. However, with God's Word the church is prepared to move forward into battle knowing that that gates of hell cannot prevail against it (see Matt. 16:18).

We are to put on each piece of armor carefully with prayer. Ephesians is characterized by prayer; so Paul exhorted his readers to enter the spiritual battle prayerfully, drawing on the available divine resource.

Southern Baptists have been characterized as people who talk a great deal about the Bible but generally know little of its contents. We can change that image by consistent, serious Bible study and by application of biblical truths to our daily living.

The Reason for the Armor

We need both the offensive and the defensive weapons because the church is in a spiritual conflict with the evil one. Satan is powerful, wicked, unscrupulous, and cunning. Christians need to know their enemy (and the enemy should not be our fellow Christians! [see Eph. 4:1-6]). In the Scriptures, the enemy is Satan and his demonic forces.

Satan is identified as "the evil one" (Eph.6:16), "the tempter" (Matt. 4:3), "the ruler of this world" (John 12:31), "the god of this world" (2 Cor. 4:4), "the prince

118

of the power of the air" (Eph. 2:2), "the
accuser of [the] brethren" (Rev. 12:10),
the one "who deceives the whole world"
(Rev. 12:9), "the ruler of the demons"
(Matt. 12:24-26), the "adversary" (1
Pet. 5:8), "the father of lies," "a
murderer" (John 8:44), and a sinner (1
John 3:8). A recognition that he is a murderer and
a liar (John 8:44) indicates that practically all forms of
evil grow out of a violation of these two things: the sacredness of life and the sacredness of truth.

In the margin, list evidences of Satan's power that you see in our world.

Satan carries out his attacks in various ways. He
counterfeits (2 Cor. 11:14-15), slanders (Gen. 3:4-5),
deceives (Rev. 20:3), blinds minds (2 Cor. 4:4), accuses
(Rev. 12:10), hinders (1 Thess. 2:18), sows tares (dar-
nel, counterfeit wheat; Matt. 13:38-39), incites persecu-
tion (Rev. 2:10), tempts to sin (Acts 5:3), and employs
evil devices (2 Cor. 2:11). His purpose is not primarily
to establish a kingdom of crime and confusion but to establish a permanent kingdom that supplants and coex-
ists with God's kingdom. He harasses God's people by
focusing attention on God's restrictions on us, which really are for our benefit. He tempts us to doubt God's
goodness. He presents attractive counterfeits for God's will and for true worship—counterfeits such as religious
power, money, position, and prestige.
He focuses our attention on the present rather than on the future values of eternity (see Heb. 12:1-2).

Do you view God's commands as restrictions or as guidelines that free us? Explain.

We must remember Satan's limita-
tions. He is accountable (Matt. 25:41). He
is neither present everywhere, all-powerful, nor
all-knowing. In light of these recognitions, we never
should underestimate him (Jude 8-9) or overestimate
him (Job 1:12). We must be on guard for attack (1 Pet.
5:8) and not invite his attacks (Eph. 4:27). We must be
aware of God's using Satan (2 Cor. 12:7), Jesus' finished work as the best defense against Satan (John

119

12:31; Rev. 12:10b-11), and Jesus' intercessory work (John 17:15). We must avail ourselves of the defense provided believers through humble submission to God (Jas. 4:6-7), the defense provided by firm resistance to Satan (Jas. 4:6-7), and the spiritual armor that God offers to His own (Eph. 6:10-18).

We are to be strong in Christ's strength and not to rely on our own self-confidence (see Eph. 6:10). We are to take seriously the stirring call to battle and we are to put on the full armor of God (see Eph. 6:11). We are to overcome the enemy through faith and to persevere by standing firm; and when we have stood, we are to continue to stand (Eph. 6:11-13). We vocally can declare our faith in Christ and openly can acknowledge Him as our Master and Lord. Christians are to confess Christ as the One who has conquered powers at the cross. We must be careful not to allow Satan to enter our lives. Thus, we should deny any allegiance to Satan, his demonic hosts, and his world. We must do this boldly and forcefully while submitting to God and drawing on His resources that He provides to resist Satan and his demonic forces.

> **Spiritual smugness is extremely dangerous. To think we are immune to common temptations and impervious to evil's assaults is to set ourselves up for a fall. Not self-reliance but dependence on God's strength will allow us to stand firm in the heat of battle.**

Communal Nature of Prayer (6:18-20)

In verses 18-20, Paul described prayer as being in the Spirit. Thus it is Spirit-taught, Spirit-energized, Spirit-enabled, and Spirit-directed. Prayer provides the pervasive atmosphere in which we take up all of the other weapons as we recognize our position in Christ.[6] Paul called for believers to pray in the Spirit. Already we have seen two examples of this kind of praying (Eph. 1:15-23; 3:14-21). Praying in the Spirit is an admission of our ignorance and a sign of our dependence on God. We come to Him saying, "Your will be done."

Prayer in the Spirit is regular and constant. This means prayer is appropriate for all occasions, when we feel like praying and when we do not. Prayer in the Spirit takes place in season and out of season; in triumph and in despair; during regular, planned times of prayer and throughout the day "without ceasing" (see 1 Thess. 5:17). Prayer takes many forms. It can be private, public, audible, or silent. It can be offered as adoration, thanksgiving, petition, or supplication. Prayer is more than talking with God; it is intimate talk with Him. It requires tenacity and endurance. Prayer requires alertness, for in prayer we experience Satan's attacks. Prayer requires concern for the entire community of faith, which means that we do not focus prayer on ourselves. Prayer should arise more out of God's Word and concern for His kingdom than out of our needs or wants.

What do you think Paul meant by "pray at all times"? What is your pattern of prayer?

Married couples need to recognize the importance of praying together.

Prayer is concerned with the church's unity, purity, and maturity (see Eph. 4:1-32). As we pray, we can expect to struggle with Satan while we remain confident of ultimate victory. This victory may come through ways unexpected in which God's grace is magnified in our lives (see 2 Cor. 12:7-9; Heb. 11:32-40). Prayer should be specific as we seek an understanding of God's way and will. Believers who pray from the heart often go through much agony in their prayers, but they never are left in agony. The reward for praying in the Spirit is the peace that passes all understanding, the interior calm that external circum-

PHOTO BY JIM WHITMER

121

stances cannot affect. Inner peace is not the goal of prayer, but it is the inevitable result.

When we enclose each part of our lives with prayer, we recognize that God is the living God who listens and acts. Somehow within the mysteries of God, He does not act in the same way if we do not pray. Yet we always must remember that we do not pray in order to get our will done in heaven but to get God's will done on earth.

Both Paul and Peter issued the command to be watchful, to stand against the evil one (see 1 Pet. 5:8). The church must watch lest savage wolves, influenced by the evil one, overtake the community and lead it astray.

In the margin, list benefits of a congregation's praying together. List two things in your church's life for which you will pray.

Paul urged the church to pray with unfailing perseverance. The actions of watchfulness and prayer are united indissolubly. Prayer is an act of vigilance, and vigilance is a result of prayer. Vigilant watchfulness is a manifestation of genuine spiritual life. It represents the church's faithfulness in avoiding being lulled into false security.

Concluding Remarks (6:21-24)

Prayer is a dominant aspect of Ephesians and is an appropriate ending for Paul. The emphasis in verses 21-24 is on prayer in the Spirit.

Paul concluded with greetings that lack the personal references usually present in his letters. This is understandable because the letter was intended to be a circular letter. Such omissions are hard to explain if the letter was intended only for the church at Ephesus, the place where Paul stayed longer than anywhere else in his ministry (see Acts 18:19-21; 19; 20:13-31). Most likely Tychicus carried the letter, along with the letter to the Colossian church and the personal note to Philemon.

Paul's concluding words underscore that the new people of God who have been granted new life and have entered into the new family still must endure spiritual warfare. Believers must take these closing exhortations seriously and arm themselves for battle in order to stand against the devil's schemes and against the evil day. We are to recognize the power available in our position in Christ and available in God's Word to live a life that is pleasing to God in faithful resistance to Satan's evil attacks.

The Letter to the Ephesians is a majestic word emphasizing that our salvation is not only for our personal benefit but also to bring praise and glory to God. We are reminded that in God's purposes, God will bring all things in the universe under Christ's rule and reign.

Paul's letter has reminded us of the church's significance as the agent of redemption on earth. In the church, God displays His manifold wisdom to all beings, including the rulers and the authorities in the heavenly realms. The church receives its purpose and power from heaven, where Christ is exalted at God's right hand. Nevertheless, the church is to live out its calling on earth as it seeks to carry out God's purposes. Christ has gifted the church to build it up in quality and in quantity and to promote unity and maturity. The church carries out its mission by evidencing a new life of purity that God's Spirit makes possible. Paul's exhortation to stand strong in the Lord still rings true, for Christ's church is involved in a great spiritual conflict; but God has given us the spiritual resources to stand in the evil day. The church, as the people of God, is to present a picture of unity. It is to exemplify Christ's ways to a watching world that longs to see the realities of the gospel lived out in authentic ways. The Letter to the Ephesians calls for the

Tychicus is one of many unsung heroes and heroines in the New Testament. Paul wrote the inspired Letter to the Ephesians, but Tychicus delivered it. How many miles did he travel? How many dangers did he face? What kept him going? Christ's cause needs the unsung heroes and heroines who are not interested in being credited but in being faithful to Christ.

What do you consider to be God's calling on your life in Christ? In what ways are you carrying out that calling?

123

church to worship, walk, witness, and be prepared for warfare as we carry out and live out God's calling on our lives in Christ.

[1]No. 8, *The Baptist Hymnal*, 1991.

[2]William Gurnall, *The Christian in Complete Armour. Or A Treatise, of the Saints War against the Devil; Wherein a Discovery is made of that Grand Enemy of GOD and his People, in his Policies, Power, Seat of his Empire, Wickedness, and chief design he hath against the Saints* (London, 1669), 31. The modern equivalent of Gurnall's work is the exposition by D. M. Lloyd-Jones, *The Christian Soldier: An Exposition of Ephesians 6:10 to 20* (Grand Rapids: Baker Book House, 1977).

[3]*Stand* is the key word of the passage. See Francis Foulkes, *The Letter of Paul to the Ephesians*, rev. ed. (Grand Rapids: Wm. B. Eerdmans Publishing Co., 1989), 178.

[4]See the background of these five pieces of armor in Archibald Thomas Robertson, "Ephesians", vol. 4 in *Word Pictures in the New Testament* (Nashville: Broadman Press, 1931), 550-51.

[5]See Harold W. Hoehner, "Ephesians," in *The Bible Knowledge Commentary* (Wheaton: Victor, 1983), 644.

[6]See E. M. Bounds, *Power through Prayer*, new ed. (Grand Rapids: Baker Book House, 1991); also John Bunyan, *The Pilgrim's Progress* (New York: Signet Classics, 1964), whose allegory follows Paul's picture of the spiritual conflict. For example, he says, "that he was forced to put up his sword, and betake himself to another weapon called all prayer" (p. 63).

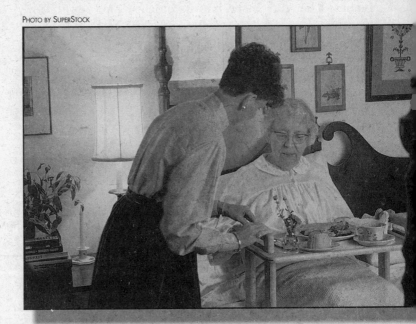

Christians have many opportunities to minister to others. What opportunities do you have?

"For He [Christ Jesus] Himself is our peace, who made both groups into one, and broke down the barrier of the dividing wall" (Eph. 2:14).

CHRISTIAN GROWTH STUDY PLAN
Preparing Christians to Grow

Answering God's call to serve Him involves preparing ourselves for the tasks He puts before us. Ephesians 4:12-13 challenges us to prepare for "works of service" and to become "mature, attaining to the full measure of the fullness of Christ" (NIV).

With today's busy lifestyles, most Christians are struggling to be prepared and mature. The challenges of our day keep us from reaching our God-given potential.

One solution to these problems is the launch of an easier-to-use Church Study Course system. This enhanced system carries the strengths of the Church Study Course system with a contemporary approach to assist church families as they move into the 21st century.

The name of the enhanced system is Christian Growth Study Plan: Preparing Christians to Serve. For information about the system, ask someone in your church office for the Christian Growth Study Plan 1996-97 Catalog. Or call the Christian Growth Study Plan Office (615/251-2525) to receive your free copy.

This book, *Ephesians: One Body in Christ* (Winter Bible Study, 1997) is a resource for course credit in the Christian Growth diploma Bible studies. The course number is CG-0106. To receive credit, read the book, complete the self-study questions, show your work to your pastor, a staff member, or church leader. Or you may read the book and participate in a group study with a minimum of 2 1/2 hours in length. Complete a Credit Request Form 725 found in the CGSP 1996-97 Catalog; then mail it to:

Christian Growth Study Plan Office
127 Ninth Avenue North, MSN 117
Nashville, TN 37234-0117
FAX: (615) 251-2525